# JUDGEMENT AT CHELMSFORD

A PAGEANT PLAY WRITTEN BY
## CHARLES WILLIAMS
[PETER STANHOPE]

*for performance at*
*The New Scala Theatre, London, W.1*
*from 23rd September to 7th October, 1939*

*in Celebration of the*
TWENTY-FIFTH ANNIVERSARY OF
## THE DIOCESE OF CHELMSFORD

GEOFFREY CUMBERLEGE
OXFORD UNIVERSITY PRESS
LONDON 1939

*First Published* - 1939

*Reprinted* - - - 1946

# PREFATORY NOTE

THE following Pageant Play was written for the twenty-fifth anniversary of the formation of the Diocese of Chelmsford, and was to have been presented, with music composed for it by Dr. Martin Shaw and under the direction of Miss Phyllis Potter, as the Director of Religious Drama in the Diocese of Chelmsford, at the Scala Theatre in London from 23 September to 7 October, 1939. The text was then ascribed to Peter Stanhope, a name which I have used elsewhere as that of a writer of verse, in order that no question of approval or disapproval of my other work might interfere with the special occasion and purpose of this.

The outbreak of war prevented the production and made vain—to that extent only—the labour which had been put into the preparation by Miss P. M. Potter and her whole company of assistants, to whom I very much desire personally to offer my profound gratitude. The courtesy they have shown and the companionship they have permitted have been throughout a shining example of that glory of love which is in the Will of Almighty God; to whom be ascribed, as is most justly due, all might, majesty, dominion and power.

CHARLES WILLIAMS.

November, 1939.

# SYNOPSIS

"JUDGEMENT AT CHELMSFORD," unlike most pageants, combines all its Episodes into a complete whole. Each, therefore, must be understood not as a separate incident, but as an incident related to all the others and to the final climax. Each episode also has, for those who care to take it so, two sides: the historical and the spiritual. Thus the complete pageant offers a representation not only of the history of the diocese, but of the movement of the soul of man in its journey from the things of this world to the heavenly city of Almighty God.

### PROLOGUE

Chelmsford, on her birthday, comes to the gate of heaven to talk with her elder brothers, the Great Sees of Christendom. There are five of these—Canterbury, Rome, Constantinople, Antioch and Jerusalem, representing the chief bishoprics of the Universal Church. Her approach is prevented by a figure called the Accuser, who warns her that before she can enter heaven she must see herself as she really is. He asks, if she were called to death and judgement that night, by the destructiveness of war, what she could say on her own behalf, and he calls on the Five Sees, ministers of justice, to listen to her defence. They enter, to the sound of aeroplanes and bombs, and also call in St. Cedd, the Apostle of Essex, to defend and befriend his spiritual child. The stage is thus set for an exhibition of her 'ways of living,' that is, how far and with what energy she has followed God.

## First Episode—Modern Times

The modern Diocese in its dual aspects of town and country life is represented by machine workers and agricultural labourers. The commonest accusation thrown at the Church is that of futility, and in this episode the accusation is presented at its face value. A young girl, eager for life, is met by a priest who, sincerely but inadequately, proposes to her the Christian religion ; she refuses it because she does not feel it to be "as strong as the blood in her." A Committee discuss ways and means of attracting the young people into the churches. A tendency arises to consider the whole world of grace in terms of the attractiveness of this world. But underneath this there remains, as the Sees point out, the undoubted power of God and the courage and faith (however badly expressed) of Christians. This episode as much as any other is therefore an assertion of Christianity.

## Episode 2—The Chelmsford Witches

The Accuser, taking advantage of this first presentation, points out the false way in which such words as Love, Power, Grace are used on earth. To exhibit this he calls up Matthew Hopkins, a lawyer of Manningtree, who under cover of the love of God, bought himself comfort by getting money for witch hunting, and shows himself as much a son of the devil as any witch. It is here that the character of the Accuser is explained. If the witches desire to see the devil, they see the Accuser in his place, for

> " God made me to be the image of each man's desire—
> A king or a poet or a devil—rarely Christ.
> Most men when at last they see their desire,
> fall to repentance—all have that chance."

The Chorus recall our Lord's saying that Satan cannot cast out Satan and mock at Satan's kingdom. Rome and Canterbury ask pardon of each other for the follies and evils done in the history of Christ's Church on earth.

### EPISODE 3—THE REFORMATION

This episode depicts the two opposing parties of Papalists and Reformers, the former fighting for the Rites and the latter for the Bible. A Catholic and a Protestant martyr are seen at the same stake. A seraph descends to release their souls to peace. They turn to each other and recognise that the mission of each was given by the other's need, and that both brought honour to Christ and joy to heaven.

### EPISODE 4—BARKING ABBEY

After the foregoing episode, Chelmsford asks to be allowed to show ordinary lives, gay as they can be, and St. Cedd calls up the girls of Barking Abbey at the Christmas feast of the Triduum, when for three days, including Holy Innocents, the girls elected their own Lady Abbess and ruled the convent as they wished. A play, supposed to be written by Nicholas Udall, one time vicar of Braintree and author of " Roister Doister," is rehearsed.

## Episode 5—John Ball and The Peasants' Rising

The Accuser enjoys as much as any the beautiful and mild moments of life, but " wit flashes to heaven more from a full stomach than ever from an empty." He accuses the Church through the ages of being negligent of man's earthly needs. He calls up the Peasants of 1431, who, inspired by the Priest, John Ball, went to King Richard to demand that the principles learnt from Holy Church should be put into practice. The needs of the poor are always the indirect, if not the direct, concern of the Church. The King fails them and they are driven back by the " wall of gold, iron and steel." As the prophets of old pronounced the doom of Babylon, so now the Chorus pronounces doom on that great city London.

" She shall stumble into the judgement away from God to feed evermore on the chaff she proffered the poor."

Chelmsford and the Great Sees join in a psalm of penitence.

## Episode 6—Martyrdom of St. Osyth

St. Cedd asserts that in spite of many fallings away from the faith, and the many times when it seemed almost to be extinguished, there have always been some who maintained belief in Love ; that is, in Love as being a real actual and dominating principle. As witness to this, St. Osyth is called from heaven. A fierce band of Danes put the nuns to flight and kill Osyth. The Chorus recall her to heaven, but Chelmsford, in need of the support of the saints, implores her to stay. Jerusalem assures her of Christ's permission, and Osyth goes to find her old homes of Essex, and many others. At this present promise of divine life, Chelmsford feels a pang of relief and understanding. She cries a little as the stress of her anxiety grows less, and she begins to believe that self-knowledge and repentance are a preliminary to the Communion of Saints.

## Episode 7—Old King Cole

The Chorus speak of the extravagance of the love of God in creating man and filling him with that same desire for extravagance of loving joy. Chelmsford proclaims that God's grace has kept joy in her, as seen in the love and friendship of man with man, woman with woman, man with woman. Legends and tales tell the same story, and she calls up " Old King Cole " (King Coel of Colchester, who was, of course, an historical character) and his daughter Helena, who, according to some legends, married Constantius, the Western Caesar, and became the mother of the first Christian Roman Emperor, Constantine the Great. Constantius discusses with King Cole the merits of the City as opposed to the Nation, and finds the City " where all nations can know themselves through others " the greater name. He admits that the one thing Rome lacks is a soul—a vision worthy of her. For the Pagan, the City and a little friendship within the City is man's total sum of good. At the sight of Helena, Love, " the only untired god that is left," reveals to him the vision that Rome lacked. To this hour of greatness he dedicates the child of the union, who, he prophesies, will draw a new doctrine into the heart of Rome. Constantinople confirms the view that the body is holy and valuable, because our Lord is incarnate and not a mirage in a desert of piety. As Moses saw the glory of God in the burning bush, so the glory of God may be revealed through " the actual unveiled beauty of flesh to eyes of love." Canterbury describes how God has been pleased to send rumours of Paradise—the invisible world of greatness—to man through his senses, and asks where witness of this may be found. Chelmsford replies that these may be found in her now as in the earliest days. The call from that other world is shrill, and whoever hears, sows a seed from Eden's giant tree of life. Man's experience is full of divine things. But, Canterbury asks, where does man reap and glean the results of these ?

It is Jerusalem who answers this question : " In me " and strangely, " in the gloom of the tomb that is no tomb." In speaking thus, Jerusalem has a deeper knowledge than the other Patriarchs, knowing that without the tomb there can be no Resurrection. He describes the violent and inflamed horror that sweeps over man, and the pain that drives along the nerves and lives of mankind, and the desolation of the soul when everything is but a vision of pain. He asks who bears witness to this. Chelmsford, too, knows the terror and the horror of life, and she knows that everyone who lives in her knows it. Remembering our Lord's promise never to fail those who call upon Him, she commands Him to come to her aid.

" Be quick, be quick ; it is I ; you love me ; come."


EPISODE 8—

St. Helena and The Invention of the Cross

As the Choir sings of the " glorious battle and the ending of the fray " Chelmsford's prayer is answered, though her struggle is not yet ended. Two seraphs descend the heavenly stairway with a covered burden. Thomas Ken, one time vicar of Little Easton, is called to explain the "mystical legend of the finding of the Cross." Preaching as to his parishioners on the day of the Invention of the Cross, he tells how St. Helena found in Jerusalem the place of the true Cross, but "find you the Cross within you, you shall find Christ Himself, so holy, so fresh, so sweet and fragrant a Cross that you shall laugh to find how you have mistook Him."

## EPILOGUE

The Chorus and Jerusalem make an impassioned appeal to Chelmsford to bend and loosen the rigid sinews of her soul. The appeal is not in vain. Chelmsford, in accepting and binding herself to the Cross, finds that grief brings joy and that peace awakes through all moments at once. Jerusalem is no longer seen as a stern father, but her final home and resting place. The Accuser is her lover, who through love of her, has made her see and face facts as they are, and brought her humble repentance. All who are in her, past, present, and to come, unite themselves to her in the great exchange of mortal and divine love through the Incarnation and Atonement. He leads her to the Great Sees, who welcome and embrace her, while the whole company sing the Te Deum "Thou art the King of Glory, O Christ" and the Diocese of Chelmsford achieves its end in God.

*PROLOGUE.*

*EPILOGUE.*

*(THE PLACE IS OUTSIDE THE GATES
OF HEAVEN, CONSIDERED AS IN THE
AIR ABOVE THE DIOCESE. CHELMSFORD
ENTERS.)*

CHELMSFORD : I am a young See, yet I am one
 with all the rest of Christendom, blest as they—
 Canterbury, Rome, Constantinople, Antioch,
 Jerusalem, my predecessors, my brothers and lords.
 My house is in the plains beyond the mouth of Thames,
 and built by the rushing wind and the tongued flames
 where the coast of heaven borders the English coast
 and the byres of Essex are the shires of the Holy Ghost.
 I am as old as the whole Church in Britain.
 Cedd raised the first rough fold of my sheep
 and I hallow his name wholesomely where the plough
 shears the fields still as in his own years,
 but otherwise now towns are much of my ministry :
 mark them, the might, mirth, and misery of England,
 spreading, treading hard on each other's heels, making me
 changed from what I was once, before the charge
 of my children was wholly mine, before the mitre
 touched my brows with something darker than age,
 to assuage their need, comfort, console, cherish,
 lest if they perish I too be cast from the place
 with my peers, the patriarchates, the heavenly thrones
 whose zones map Christendom, in England, and beyond
 where the great ships float from my river. To-day
 the fledged heel of Contemplation strikes the edged wheel
 of Time, to spin it, and heaven opens within.
 It is my birthday ; on this feast I come to the place
 of grace in vision, to the gate of heaven, to walk

and talk with the grand celestial princes, they
who assess the deeds of the Church militant on earth,
and confess in clear light the fulfilment of their needs.
I am come shyly to meet them ; blessed be he
who made me also in Christendom holy and free.

>            (*A KIND OF GENTLE DISCORD. THE
>            ACCUSER COMES IN.*)

THE ACCUSER : Halt there, sweet !
CHELMSFORD :                          Whose feet here
    interpose between me and those who await me ?
THE ACCUSER : Child of the Apostles, do you hope to come
    quite so easily into heaven ? think again.
    The Apostolic Sees will have something to say
    to that ; and I too, whether they do or not.
CHELMSFORD : Who are you ? where do you come from ?
THE ACCUSER :                          I come
    from going with time up and down the earth,
    testing the worth of the confessors. David and Job,
    Peter and Paul, Becket and Wesley knew me ;
    there are few who do not. The Creator of all,
    Primal Wisdom, primal Justice, primal Love,
    made me and bade me to my work. I stand
    at the right hand of all men in their hour of death ;
    but also they may see me at any hour. Their breath
    catches, their blood is cold, they remember their sins.
    They see what they have made of their lives.
CHELMSFORD :                          But why
    to me now, to-day, at the gate of heaven ?
THE ACCUSER : Sweet, your world is become perilous to you.
    This is no age with long peaceful hours
    fastidiously changing young things into old ;
    families, cities, churches gradually thriving
    through the happy quiet virtues, as the corn grows.
    The air is dangerous with flames other than Pentecost

and a host other than angelic rides—hark !
>(*THE NOISE OF AEROPLANES AT A
DISTANCE.*)

Day and dark alike carry the things
that strike bitterly and awfully at bed and board
leaving the dead in the shelters and in the streets.
Hark !
>(*THE DISTANT SOUND OF BOMBS ; A FAINT
SCREAM OR TWO. AEROPLANES.*)

If you were called to-night to be judged, how
could you answer ? do not speak ; I have come to show.
>(*THE AEROPLANES SEEM TO PASS OVER.*)

CHELMSFORD : I take refuge with God.

THE ACCUSER :                    So do ; but I too,
>I shall be there.  Call on your refuge, call.
>I will call for you.  Ho, heavens of creation,
>ho, ministers of justice, vengeance, mercy,
>ho, foundations of grace ; come down and hear.

CHELMSFORD : Mercy of God, justify me.

THE ACCUSER :                    Truth of God,
>exhibit her !
>>(*THE CHORUS WITHOUT BEGINS THE* DIES
IRAE *INTERRUPTED BY THE BOMBS.*)

THE CHORUS : Dies irae.........................
>(*THE PROCESSION OF THE SEES, ACCOM-
PANIED BY MUSICIANS AND CANDLE-
BEARERS. WHEN THEY HAVE TAKEN
THEIR PLACES THEY SPEAK.*)

CANTERBURY : I am Canterbury ; Augustine taught me ;
beside Augustine
>I gathered to myself the fruits of Iona and Glastonbury ;
>I have fathered many children ; you, daughter,
>loved as much as any.  I will know what you know.

ROME : I am Rome ; Peter made me and blessed Paul ;

no small history is mine, and yet all
is to be the servant of servants and intercede
as Peter at need was lamb-like bidden to do.

CONSTANTINOPLE : I am Constantinople ; I raised
a Church to Holy Wisdom ; it turned to a mosque.
The East famished ; the West forgot ; but God
discerned through all how I praised the Unity.

ANTIOCH : Antioch am I ; in me the faithful were named
Christian first, shamed a little in the naming,
a scandal to others. O Christians, are you to yourselves
a scandal now ? or by yourselves unblamed ?

JERUSALEM : I am the oldest and youngest of all the Sees,
Jerusalem ; the body of my Bishop was never shrined
after it was twined on the criss-cross pontifical chair,
and a mitre there of a sharp kind on his head.

ALL THE SEES (stretching their arms upwards and outwards
to touch their fingers) :
Blessed and hallowed and praised be the Thing in us
communicating each to other and other to each,
Blessed and hallowed and praised in the beginning
and in the ending be God, in time and beyond time.

CANTERBURY : Daughter, when Contemplation called to us
that you were waiting at the gate of the third heaven
we arose and came ; the fame of all the bishoprics
comes up to us ; we have loved you much
for the souls that sprang into heaven by the touch
that took from our own the power of your hand ; and
   the speech of your voice
that learned to teach others as we taught you.
But it seems the Accuser of all things, living and dead,
the dweller on the threshold of love, is here too,
new-set to hinder and hamper your coming.

THE ACCUSER : Neither to hamper nor hinder ; I show fact
outward and inward. It is her business

if the facts of her history rise between her and you
to shut the gate of heaven in her face, and her fate
leaves her outside.

CANTERBURY :  When the High God made you,
brother, he bade you interpret in your fashion—
the worst of the worst ; accuracy without compassion,
curst things always shown as guilt—
often, not always, they are.  Call some other,
some friend of our child, to show the other side
of truth : even truth has always two sides.

THE ACCUSER : Call anyone you like ; call all you can.
I desire neither her damnation nor her salvation.
Sister, who will you have to defend and befriend you ?

CHELMSFORD : Who more than he who first taught me ?
brought my shires through the shining water
into Christendom ? these places that were I
before I was named ? shamed though I be
for ill following his way, yet am I still
his mystical child.  Blessed one, blessed Cedd,
sped long since to your saving, to the Prince of Zion,
cry to your Lord that he send you down now ;
how should he be content to let you lose
your love's effort, the incarnate news of grace ?
Cedd, come from Christ, come once more
to this shore betwixt earth and heaven ; speak for me.

THE ACCUSER : Come, listen to the world in which you lived.
Christendom has thrived well since you died,
in some thirteen hundred years to rend the sky
with flaming fleets, and the streets shrieking below.
O it has made a good thing of your speaking.
            (*THE AEROPLANES AND BOMBS* : *ST. CEDD
            ENTERS.*)

ST. CEDD : I was with holy Aidan, come from Iona,
lord of Lindisfarne in the spiritual land :

the cry reached me there, now as before,
when the East Saxons called ; then being thralled
in a sacred servitude to Aidan my overlord,
I was sent by him to lead a raid into Essex ;
I obeyed ; forest and ford heard the sound
of the northern sea of Christ crying *Alleluia*.
So there we stamped the sacraments on them.
At Maldon and Tilbury I made a house of monks
to be hosts of adoration, nor forget I
the vows between me and my folk, the yoke we carry
each for other : what was spoke then
lasts while men do, on earth or in heaven,
liege of lastingness, sworn faith of the Saviour.
What may I do now for England and Essex ?
Say, pontiffs, say, child of love.
Say you also, well-belovèd brother,
who have of all tasks the ungratefullest toil.

THE ACCUSER : Cedd, we have often met, and now again.
Neither can grudge other, but that these
may judge rightly, do what you can and may.
Explain, as best, what has happened in Essex
since your day ended : your daughter is mitred,
very princely, prinked in modest pomp,
habitually sedate in her seat along the water.
Good ; I will show you her soul—

CHELMSFORD :                                         Ah no !

THE SEES : Show ; show ; show ; show ; show—

THE ACCUSER : Her history, her ways of living.

ST. CEDD :                                         Show.

THE ACCUSER : Sweet, what say you ? judgement or no
   judgement ?

CHELMSFORD (after a silent horror) : I have believed ; I take
   refuge with God ; show.

THE ACCUSER : See then ; this is your belief in God.

17

(*THE SOUND OF AEROPLANES AGAIN, BUT THIS TIME, INSTEAD OF FADING, IT CHANGES INTO A LOUDER NOISE WHICH DEVELOPS INTO THE HUM OF MACHINES AND THE CLANG OF STEEL. THERE RISES OUT OF IT A SONG. THE MACHINE-WORKERS ENTER ON ONE SIDE; ON THE OTHER THE AGRICULTURAL LABOURERS. THE SONG IS ACCOMPANIED BY A MECH-ANICAL DANCE. WHEN IT STOPS, THE LABOURERS BEGIN THEIR DANCE. A YOUNG MAN AND A GIRL BREAK AWAY FROM THEM SUDDENLY.*)

*The Song.*

Belly is barking, barking aloud,
    Lacking a good square meal.
Fire him and fill him, fatten him well,
    Stodge up the stiff on steel—

THE GIRL : This isn't the kind of life I want.

THE MACHINE WORKERS (in a subdued murmur) : This wasn't the kind of life we wanted.

THE LABOURERS : This wasn't the kind of life we wanted.

THE GIRL : I'm not going to live in this end-of-the-world pig-sty all my days. Can't you get a job in the town? There's a noise there.

THE YOUNG MAN (more doubtfully): I might; I don't know. It's not easy to get a job.

THE MACHINE WORKERS: It's not easy to keep a job.

THE LABOURERS: It's not easy to live by your job.

THE GIRL: I can—in the factories. My sister's got one and she and her boys have something like a time. Couldn't we—*darling*?

> (*SHE HANGS ON HIM AND CAJOLES HIM. HE LOOKS OVER TO THE MACHINES.*)

THE YOUNG MAN: We might try.

> (*THEY MOVE A LITTLE; THE MACHINES BREAK OUT; HE HESITATES; THE GIRL DRAGS HIM ON.*)

THE GIRL: Hark! Come on, come on! That's life, that is!

> (*A PRIEST APPEARS NEAR THEM.*)

THE PRIEST: Our Lord said: ' I am come that you might have life and that you might have it more abundantly.' Think a little of what this means. It is no good looking for life in the loud streets of our large towns with their showy lights—that is not the kind of life you want. The kind of life you want is the quiet life that is found in the peaceful heart—and how do we find that? That is what the Church can tell you. A little self-denial, a little attention to—

THE GIRL: I've had a packet of self-denial ever since I was born, it's time someone else had a turn. And when I want more life—and don't I?—it's not in churches on Sunday evenings I'm going to look for it. No (she chokes back the adjective) fear!

THE YOUNG MAN (more politely): Some other day perhaps, sir, if you'll excuse us. I've got to see about getting a job now.

THE PRIEST : Yes, of course.  Only after all we do want something to fall back on, don't we ? something to keep you straight in your job and to keep you happy outside your job.  Something everlastingly good.  Our Lord wanted the young people to be happy and………

THE GIRL : Did he ?  I can tell you one thing, if he thought singing hymns was the thing a girl wanted to keep her happy, he was a good way off.  When the heart's kicking in me and my throat's dry, and that fellow and the other fellow, what good are hymns going to be then ?  they're nothing to bite on.  Jesus ! what do you know about it ?  Don't do this and don't do that and you don't want a noise—I do want a noise, I want a noise as loud as the blood in me ; I mean to make a fight of it and give as good as I get— or very nearly ; and that's what I'm out for and that's what I'm going to have, so there's for your church-going and your don't, don't, don't.  Come on, *darling*.

THE YOUNG MAN : Excuse us, sir.

> (*THE TWO OF THEM REACH THE MACHINE CIRCLE ; AS THEY DO SO, THE DANCE (ON BOTH SIDES) BEGINS AGAIN. THE YOUNG MAN IS KNOCKED DOWN BY A HAMMER, AND HIS BODY IS FLUNG OUT. THE GIRL GIVES A SCREAM, BUT SHE IS CAUGHT UP IN THE DANCE, AND WHIRLED ROUND. THE PRIEST LOOKS ROUND AND BECKONS. THE MEMBERS OF A COMMITTEE APPEAR AND JOIN HIM.  THE DANCE CEASES.*)

THE PRIEST : Ladies and gentlemen, fellow-Christians !  It's very kind of you to come to this meeting.  The subject to-night is *What can we do to get the people into our Churches* ?  I'm sure this is a very urgent question nowadays when Communism and Fascism are making such inroads. And Science—not that I'm against Science, for after all where should we be without it ? But we ought to be attracting the young, and we don't seem to be attracting them as much as we might wish.

A WELL-MEANING LADY : I think the music's too solemn ; we want brighter tunes.

A FIRM MAN : We want to make them *welcome* ; we're too standoffish.

THE PRIEST : But how can one welcome them if they're not there to welcome ?

THE FIRM MAN : Welcome them first and then they'll come. Brotherly love. Joy.

(*HE PRACTISES A CHEERFUL SMILE.*)

A CRITICAL LADY : Too much excitement—that's what's the matter with them. Look at the books they read and look at the films they see and look at the dog-races !

AN EAGER MAN (breaking in) : Yes, but why not give them these things *in* the churches instead of outside ?

THE PRIEST (startled) : What, dog-races ? O really, no-one's more anxious than I am to find some way of getting into their—shall we say hearts ? but I don't think we could have dog-races.

THE WELL-MEANING LADY : Not up the aisles !

THE EAGER MAN : Well, I don't say *dog-races* exactly, but that's the kind of thing you've got to compete with, and that's what we've got to realize. Show them the Church wants *them*. Other days, other ways. In the Dark Ages it was different ; everyone went to church because there wasn't anywhere else to go. Now there is.

ANTIOCH : There were a good many other places to go to in my time. But we managed.

THE FIRM MAN : I agree with this lady ; we want to make the services brighter. Brighter tunes—and more candles. And perhaps even a little incense—quietly, of course.

Nothing to show. There's something about the *smell* of incense that's attractive.

THE WELL-MEANING LADY : I don't think candles are much of a draw nowadays—not with the electric light everywhere.

THE FIRM MAN (proceeding) : And no sermons.

A CURATE : There I think you're wrong. We want more sermons—more sound doctrine. Modernism is ruining lives.

THE CRITICAL LADY : There's not much doctrine I hear that I can approve of. It's all High Church or Low Church or Broad Church or something. Teach them to be honest and punctual and clean—that's what we want them to be, and it's what they want to be themselves if they only knew.

THE WELL-MEANING LADY : Yes—isn't it a pity they don't seem to know ?

THE CURATE : The Church is not meant chiefly to teach morals.

THE CRITICAL LADY : More's the pity.

(*THE PRIEST HASTILY SUPPRESSES THE INDIGNANT CURATE.*)

THE FIRM MAN : The trouble is that all these extra things cost money, and we can't afford it. As it is, even after the jumble sale, we're in debt. Whereas a cheerful smile doesn't cost anything.

THE WELL-MEANING LADY : O don't you think so ?

THE CRITICAL LADY : It does if it's due to drink, as it often is.

THE EAGER MAN : Now, there you are. Why not have a Bottle Service ? They have Bottle Parties ; why not a Bottle Service ? I don't say *in* the Church ; why not in the Parish Hall ? and everyone bring his own bottle, and have a really splendid time. Lemonade or beer or even cold tea.

THE CURATE : The Church is not a drinking club.

THE EAGER MAN : No—but why not make it one ?

>    (*THE COMMITTEE BECOME AGITATED.*)

THE PRIEST : Well, we must think it over, think it over. I think the discussion has not been without its point, and I'm very gratful for this friendly co-operation. Now, before we break up, just to encourage ourselves as I may say, shall we sing *Onward, Christian Soldiers* ?

>    (*THEY BEGIN. AFTER ABOUT THREE LINES THE NOISE OF THE MACHINES JOINS IN AND PRESENTLY DOMINATES THE TUNE. THE DANCE BEGINS AGAIN ; THIS TIME THE MACHINE-WORKERS ENLARGE THEIR MOVEMENTS TILL THEY ABSORB THE COMMITTEE—EXCEPT FOR THE PRIEST— AND THE YOUNGER OF THE LABOURERS ; THE OLDER ONES DISAPPEAR. THE DANCE BECOMES MORE AUTOMATIC, AND AT LAST THE DANCERS MOVE OFF MECHANICALLY. AS THE SOUND DIES AWAY, THE AERO-PLANES ARE AGAIN HEARD.*)

THE PRIEST : Well, perhaps it is a little disheartening, but one must just go on. Our Lord didn't come in vain— we know that.

>    (*HE BEGINS TO SING* ONWARD, CHRISTIAN SOLDIERS *AGAIN BY HIMSELF. THE BOMBS ARE HEARD. HE STARTS, BUT PULLS HIMSELF UP ; THE LIGHT FADES A LITTLE AND IN A KIND OF DUSK HE MOVES OFF, HIS SOLITARY VOICE DEFYING THE DESTRUCTIVENESS OF THE WORLD. THE ACCUSER BEGINS TO SPEAK BUT IS INTERRUPTED.*)

CONSTANTINOPLE : And the odd thing is—that he is quite right.

THE ACCUSER (passionately) : This then, Christians, is your exhibition
    to-day of what once—you say—happened,
    the alteration of the whole world's orbit, souls
    caught in the thunderstorm of grace and so struck
    by the luck of the heavenly lightning that their branded flesh
    loosed their expanded spirits into the air
    of Christ's ascension ; on earth they were dead to earth
    being by a new birth remade into passion—
    And this now is the latest fashion of the glory
    that burns at every point in man and yearns
    to escape, will he yield it way, into the strong
    radiance of Christ in him and he in the world.
    Sweet, was Christ crucified to create this chat ?
    some other, less notable, sacrifice might have served.

CANTERBURY : This is indeed your habit, brother ; often
    through many centuries I have heard you talk so :
    I know your plausible tongue ; it has trapped many.
    Yes, certainly ; this is the creation of Christ—
    more foolish than need be, selfish often, often
    misguided, slothful ; but it is this or the world—

THE ACCUSER : Let her answer ; this is she ; can she at this gate of heaven
    honestly believe she is not the same as the world ?
    She loses her children daily and gains none ;
    she refuses to understand her own gospel ;
    she prefers always the second-best.  You (to Chelmsford),
    answer : since you have failed neatly to slip,
    without being exposed completely, into divinity,
    answer : what is the difference between you and the world ?

CHELMSFORD (faltering) : I do not know......I see I am poorer than I thought.

CANTERBURY : Any of us could answer for her ; do you,
    Cedd, son of Christ, show us some other vision.
ST. CEDD : God, for his reasons, did not choose to bless
    everyone with the violence of grace ; the world's axis
    was not turned as the temple veil was torn,
    whirled into wisdom. Rather, as boys toil
    to raise a pole too heavy for their hands and backs,
    the common people, age by age, were bid
    struggle against hell to set up heaven :
    if they have not stormed the frontier of one kingdom
    they have been recalled from the worst edge of the other.
    The common people are the brightness and darkness of
      existence,
    since God chose to bid Adam multiply—
    not heroes, geniuses, saints. Folly and foulness
    have they in plenty, and plentifully practise love.
    They are each a category of Christ's own identity
    which they can turn to Antichrist. It is no small thing
    that love should work so steadily in their lives.
THE ACCUSER : Love ?
ST. CEDD : Love.
THE ACCUSER : Curiously are heavenly names
    used on earth—love, power, grace.
    Have you ever heard in your heaven of Matthew Hopkins
    who between the first King Charles and the second
    in the towns of England traded foul bargains
    in stuff of evil no less detestable than he ?
    He bought himself comfort by hunting the covetousness
      of others.
    See in him and in the dark devices he harried
    how wildly the imagination in Christian lands
    loosed itself into a lurking delirium,
    and the witch-hunters ran with the witches through the
      ditches of the soul.

(ELIZABETH CLARKE AND AN IMP WITH
A TOAD'S HEAD ENTER ON ONE SIDE AND
SEEM TO SLEEP. ON THE OTHER MATTHEW
HOPKINS AND JOHN STEARNE ENTER.)

HOPKINS : Master Stearne, Master Stearne, now we must be busy. The Lord has called us to discoveries.

STEARNE : Sir, he has blessed you greatly ; he has made of you an instrument of salvation against hell.

HOPKINS : Yes. I think he has. He would not have me be a lawyer ; no-one came to my house at Ipswich. I waited all day and caught nothing, and then I came to Manningtree and waited, and still I caught nothing. There are too many lawyers in these parts, and the fees that the people pay them are very paltry. I could get no reasonable living here.

STEARNE : Sir, it was the Lord's working that you should be his chosen vessel.

HOPKINS : Yes—yes, certainly. Certainly it was the remarkable work of the Lord. I see a way opening that shall be popular and profitable to me—as his servant, of course, as his servant. It is written that they shall not muzzle the ox that treads out the corn.

STEARNE : I have thought often that I sniffed hell in the streets. Essex is a devil's parlour for witchcraft.

HOPKINS : It is fortunate that I should choose a house so near their parlour. I have been awakened by their voices night after night.

STEARNE : Sir, it is the Lord's doing and it is marvellous in our eyes. Sir, give him the glory.

HOPKINS : So I do, so I do. But we must honour the poor vessel he uses ; we must pay it respect and keep it— polished, as I may say. Good John, we must not forget that they who serve the altar should live by the altar. I do not mean it papistically. I hope the magistrates are godly men ; they shall have profit to their souls if they spend well now. My costs will be high if I am to search out this iniquity to its conclusion. I must be highly advanced—for the Lord's sake, John, for the Lord's sake.

STEARNE : Sir, we are all altogether abominable to him except in the mystery of his predestination—

HOPKINS : Yes, that is what I say—his predestination ; that is what I say—he predestinated me to be a remarkable finder of witches. I am a man of no learning, it is true ; I have not read many wise books ; I do not know what they did in France and High Germany. I am a simple man, good John, but I hope I can recognise evil when other people commit it : the Lord bless us all ! Have you warned the magistrates and the soldiers ?

STEARNE : Sir, they are waiting for us ; when I call them they will come.

HOPKINS : It is time then ; come this way. I have made a little opening into the room. Don't be afraid, John : the devil will not hurt us.

STEARNE : Sir, our Lord's hand is over all His saints.

(*THEY SETTLE DOWN TO WATCH. THE IMP NUDGES CLARKE.*)

THE IMP : Mistress, mistress ; it is time, mistress.

CLARKE : Aigh, aigh, it is time. Aigh, chuck ; precious chuck to wake me !

THE IMP : Give me a sup of blood, mistress.

CLARKE : Little glutton, little glutton !
        (*SHE LETS HIM SUCK.*)

THE IMP : Ai, ai. (It runs about.)

CLARKE : Little sweet imp. Here ! (She speaks in his ear).
Will *he* come tonight ? will he ? Ann West is bringing
her daughter at last ; will *he* come ?

THE IMP : Do I know, mistress ? Here again and gone again
and one in the corner to be cold in the vitals ; is she
pretty ? is she young ? is she neat for him and meat for
him ? he will not come for nothing. Ai, ai : who is at the
door, mistress, who is at the door ?
        (*A KNOCK. CLARKE GOES, AND AN IMP
        WITH A CAT'S HEAD RUNS IN, THEN ANN
        LEACH.*)

LEACH : I wouldn't shut the door, Elizabeth ; there are others
coming. Mistress Gooding is at the corner, and I saw
three shadows beyond her. They'll all be here soon. It's
a cold night.
        (*THE IMPS SIT DOWN IN THE SHADOWS
        AT THE BACK. THE MUSIC GROWS
        STRONGER. A KNOCK. CLARKE GOES.
        GOODING ENTERS ; HER IMP SLIPS IN
        AFTER HER ; IT HAS A KID'S HEAD.*)

GOODING : Where is she ?

LEACH : Who ?

GOODING : Who ? the girl ! Where is she ? where is she ?
isn't she here ? isn't she coming ?

CLARKE : No need to be so vexed ; her mother's bringing her.
She'll be here without doubt, for she met me in the
market this morning and said she to me : ' Goody Clarke,
Goody Clarke, shall I be made a witch tonight ? ' ' You
shall that, my maid,' said I, ' to go with your mother
wherever you will, and not sitting at home with toad in
its hole till she comes back.' And then she looked so

and she smiled *so*, and all sideways—*so* ; she'll be a fine one.

EACH : They've stopped maybe by Farmer Edwards' house to oversee his daughter again : he was bitter enough once to all of us, but now his child is mazed this sennight, and her eyes rolling. Horses, cows, child. (She leans to Clarke.) Will *he* be here ?

> (*A KNOCK : THE DOOR FLIES OPEN ; ANN WEST AND HER DAUGHTER REBECCA ARE SEEN. THEY COME IN. THE MUSIC TAKES CHARGE. THE FOUR WITCHES BOB AT EACH OTHER, REBECCA STANDING STILL BY HER MOTHER, WHO PRESENTLY LAYS A FINGER ON HER DAUGHTER'S LIP AND SEEMS TO BID HER GO AND SIT ON THE FLOOR WITH THE IMPS. SHE DOES SO. THE WITCHES, GOODING DIRECTING, BRING OUT A BRAZIER AND THROW IN HERBS ; AFTERWARDS, BEHIND IT, TWO BLACK CANDLES, WHICH THEY LIGHT FROM THE BRAZIER. THE WITCHES KNEEL ROUND THE BRAZIER AND SING. PRESENTLY A KIND OF GREEN LIGHT FLASHES UP. THE WITCHES RISE AND BEGIN TO MOVE ROUND THE BRAZIER FROM RIGHT TO LEFT AGAINST THE SUN ; THEY WALK ONE AFTER THE OTHER, BUT HOLDING HANDS : THEIR MOTION BECOMES QUICKER TILL THEY ARE ALMOST RUNNING. THE FORE-MOST, WHOSE HAND IS STRETCHED IN FRONT OF HER, CRIES OUT*) :*

HE WITCH : The hand ! the hand ! he has me.

HE OTHER WITCHES : Ha, master !

> (*THE DANCE BECOMES VERY FAST FOR A*

> MOMENT OR TWO AND CEASES. TH.
> WITCHES BREAK OFF AND STAND AS I.
> WORSHIPPING. THEN THEY REVIVE AN.
> GO BETWEEN THE BRAZIER AND TH.
> CANDLES.)

GOODING (between the candles) : The girl.

ANN WEST : Rebecca.

> (REBECCA GOES ROUND THE STAGE AN.
> COMES TO THE BRAZIER. THE MUSI.
> CEASES, THE LIGHT DISAPPEARS AN.
> ILLUMINATES THE UPPER STAGE.)

ANITOCH : England, I see, has not forgot the things
that once were done in me by different rites,
altars, rich lamps, balsams, and thuribles,
magical summons to the heart to express death ;
before the apostolic trumpet shook
the image the necromancers sought to look on.
But this is under the apostolic shield ;
how comes this, daughter ?

CHELMSFORD : This was here before
ever the Cross grew on the English shore ;
this is the seed of Eden under the curse,
and he, he waters it ; it is his work.

THE ACCUSER : Not much mine either. I have done no
worse
than to exhibit to men their own desires,
their love, their hunger, their hold on hell. If
they strongly deceive their bodies with their hope
they see me in the image of false belief ,
as these perhaps this night.. You Christians,
you are not responsible for hell, but only
for how you help high heaven to deal with hell
whether in a hellish way or in a heavenly.
See how you did once.

HOPKINS : It is time now. We shall catch them in their own
    pestilential wickedness : let us bring the guard in on
    them.

STEARNE : Sir, will you not stay while I fetch the guard?
    If you could testify that you had seen the Prince of the
    Power of the Air—

HOPKINS : No, no. Good John, we have seen enough. They
    will tell us everything presently. Come, fetch the guard
    and godly men.

        *(THEY SLIP OUT.)*

        *(THE LIGHT APPEARS AGAIN ON THE*
        *LOWER STAGE. THE GIRL IS NOW IN HER*
        *WHITE SHIFT ; THE BRAZIER IS MOVED*
        *AND SHE KNEELS IN ITS PLACE. GOODING*
        *IS STILL BETWEEN THE CANDLES. SHE*
        *SPEAKS, IN A VOICE QUITE UNLIKE HER*
        *OWN.)*

GOODING : Do you renounce your baptism?
        *(THE GIRL BENDS FORWARD : GOODING*
        *PINCHES OUT THE CANDLES. THE MUSIC*
        *BEGINS : GOODING CALLS ABOVE IT.)*

GOODING : Jarmara, Pechin, Panu !
        *(THE IMPS RUN FORWARD. TWO OF THEM*
        *CATCH THE GIRL'S HANDS AND HOLD*
        *THEM OUT : THE OTHER GOES TO GOODING,*
        *WHO KISSES HIM AND GIVES HIM A THIN*
        *KNIFE. HE RUNS ROUND BEHIND THE*
        *GIRL AND SEEMS TO PRICK HER : SHE*
        *SCREAMS.)*

ALL THE WITCHES AND IMPS : Witch's mark, witch's mark,
    witch's mark !
        *(THE GIRL KISSES THE IMPS ; SHE LEAPS*
        *UP, AND DANCES WITH THEM. THEN THE*
        *WITCHES SET THE GIRL BEFORE THE*

*CANDLES WHICH ARE AGAIN LIT AND*
*STAND BEHIND HER. THEY PRESENT A*
*CEREMONY OF INVOCATION. AS THEY*
*CROUCH AT ONE POINT THE MUSIC*
*PAUSES, AND THE VOICE OF THE*
*ACCUSER SAYS:*

THE ACCUSER : Little time is left them now,
    before the gallows is built and the pyre ; in their fire
    they shall have this single help : they shall see me.
    God made me to be the image of each man's desire—
    a king or a poet or a devil—and rarely Christ.
    Most men when at last they see their desire,
    fall to repentance—all have that chance.

        *(HE GOES DOWN, AND SUDDENLY AS THE*
        *LIGHT BECOMES BRIGHT IS SEEN STAND*
        *ING BETWEEN THE CANDLES. THE GIRL*
        *FALLS FLAT ; THE WITCHES CRY OUT*
        *THERE IS A GREAT KNOCKING AT THE*
        *DOOR. THE LIGHTS COME FULLY ON*
        *THERE IS A NOISE OF A BREAKING DOOR*
        *AND THE MAGISTRATES, SOLDIERS, AND*
        *STEARNE ENTER. THE IMPS SLIP AWAY*
        *THE WITCHES RUN ABOUT IN DISORDER*
        *AND ARE SEIZED AND BOUND. HOPKINS*
        *COMES IN.)*

HOPKINS : Hold them, hold them. Have them away. Let
them be watched tonight ; let them be run to and fro
about the room and have no rest, that, being kept
awake, they may be the more active to call their imps
and familiars the sooner to help and hearten them. Let
them not lie down or so much as sit in a chair ; and for
the better effecting it, get others to help you, and change
among yourselves two or three times an hour, and let
some watch the doors and walls, and if you see a spider

or any such vermin about the room, kill it, but if you
can by no means come at it to kill it, then take note that
it is his shape who comes to them, and you may know that
he is confounded by cause that his firebrand darlings
are put away from him. Watch and walk them! watch
and walk them.

THE MAGISTRATE : Sir, the town is in your debt tonight.
This is a very awful thing that such devilish practices
should go on so near us. I have heard that children have
been overlooked by them and are near sick to death.

HOPKINS : It is my calling ,sir. I have it in mind to go through
all these counties, through Essex and Suffolk, and
wherever good pious folk ask me, to find what evil is
done. Sir, it is a holy thing to seek after the evil that
other folk commit—but, sir, it needs money. Proof is
dear and travelling is dear.

THE MAGISTRATE : I will speak of it to the Council ; we must
not miss the salvation of the Lord. But as for these—

> (*THE WITCHES ARE RUN TO AND FRO.
> PRESENTLY THEY COLLAPSE, EXCEPT THE
> GIRL WHO SEEMS ALL THIS WHILE TO BE
> IN A KIND OF TRANCE. THERE IS FINALLY
> A PROCESSION ACROSS THE STAGE, WHILE
> A LURID LIGHT, AS OF FIRE, GLOWS
> EVERYWHERE.*)

THE ACCUSER : Fire always over Christendom, always fire !
How shall God not require the ashes at your hands,
patriarchs ? ashes of burned men, when
you swerved from the Will to keep the word, when
you abandoned God's heart for the philosophical art
of argument, and outraged men's bodies to save their
souls,
lacking love's decencies ! fire over Christendom, fire !
Protestants at Smithfield, Jesuits at Tyburn, fire !

and at Colchester the hid school from overseas
toiled for the Religion, while the last abbot
died for the Faith—fire over Christendom, fire !
Will you destroy Satan by the help of Satan ?
or establish Christ by shedding the blood of Christ ?

JERUSALEM : Satan falls always by his own divisions
but the blood of Christ being shed brings forth Christ.

THE CHORUS : When the Jews came forth to accuse Messias
he answered them riddling, playing with words,
saying : ' If Satan cast out Satan,
if hell be divided to ruin hell,
tell me, can Satan's kingdom stand ? '

Lord, let thy children now let show
the answer the Jews seemed not to know,
losing their heads in their eager rage ;
now let thy servants answer unchid :
' Lord, whoever supposed it did ? '

Let the angelic armies smile,
seeing it topple all the while :
' How shall Satan's kingdom stand ?
Lord, it crashes on either hand,
and where is its substance of delight ? '

JERUSALEM : Yet here and now, for the follies and evils
done in the history of Christ's Church on earth,
reconcile we again ourselves to each other.

CANTERBURY (to Rome) : Brother, we have exchanged too
much pain ;
Once more I entreat your pardon—without condition.
But if it should please you now to do so too
we might begin a new revision of Christendom.

ROME (to Canterbury) : Ah brother, well may I seek pardon
from all Christendom for that which weak men
and wicked, or rash saints even, have done in my name.

34

The immaculate doctrine is wounded seven times by their shame.

CANTERBURY (embracing): Blessed be God that pardon is laughter in heaven.

ROME (embracing): And the laughter pierces to degrees seventy-times-seven.

ANTIOCH: Pardon is love-in-freedom and pardon pierces
—since first men were called Christians in me—
down to new delight and new love
which else in the hard surface could not grow:
what did one of your own poets say?

THE CHORUS: 'Thus through all eternity
        I forgive you, you forgive me;
        as our dear Redeemer said—
        this the wine and this the bread.'

CHELMSFORD: Bring us, my lords, to look, forgiving and forgiven,
on the trouble of our honour that shall be joy in heaven.
When one for the Bible and another for the Church fought
and still Christ from either his own honour brought.

(*A ROYAL PURSUIVANT ENTERS, WITH AN OFFICER.*)

THE PURSUIVANT : Go, seek ; if you hear woman or man speak
of this English Bible, have an eye on them.
There are who about Colchester and Essex ply
Tyndale's trade in heresy ; go—watch.
His brother lives hereabouts ; watch carefully.
Catch as catch can—and take all the haul to the Bishop.

(*THEY GO OUT SEPARATELY. A MAN AND WOMAN ENTER.*)

THE MAN : I have a copy of it here ; I bought it in London.
I can read a little in it, and our vicar more,
wonderful new things, as true as Christ,
as strange as grace, and as strong as the heart's stir.

THE WOMAN : Hide it, be careful ; must you dally with death ?
Why not be content with what your mother
taught you, a child, and I teach our children ?
no, you must have some bravery, some bold danger ;
what will happen to our babies if you are hanged ?

THE MAN : Wit may hide it well ; have no fear.
But the Bishop shall whistle in vain ; it has come to abide,
swimming up Thames with the tide against the river
from Germany and the Low Countries ; a wind shall blow
in the flame of the spirit against their corrupt rites,

and the bishops may try to clutch lightning as well as
this.
They will burn all they find ; it has such a touch
to cleanse their poisonous doll-dusty air ;
and there they will be again, back at the beginning
with God and the Bible always winning against them.
It is indeed a New Testament to us.

THE WOMAN : I do not know but the old things were best.
Those changes of heart bring bitterness everywhere.
My gossip's brother has become a hot gospeller,
and none in her house have had quiet hours since.
I think our Lord did not mean us to be so pious
as to interfere with the day's brewing and churning.

THE OFFICER (running in and calling—as the Pursuivant re-
enters on the other side) :
Sir, have you heard the Abbot is caught for treason ?

THE PURSUIVANT : He said that all the water of Thames
would not wash
the King's Majesty of covetousness—false traitor !
He......ha, sir, what book is that you have ?

THE MAN : Sir, what is that to you ? it is no evil,
though maybe Antichrist, were he here, might think so.

THE PURSUIVANT : Sir, by your leave : we carry the King's
commission
to examine all books ; there are eggs that hatch
vipers out to-day in the Essex sun.

THE MAN : Nay, I will match you for that ; there are a fine
brood
of adders snuffing incense and—

THE PURSUIVANT : Do you say so, friend ?
Show it ; nay, do you tussle ? I will mend you for that.
(HE CATCHES THE BOOK. THE WOMAN
SCREAMS.)

THE WOMAN : O blessed mother of mercy, help us all !

*(THE MAN AND THE PURSUIVANT WHEEL
ROUND, CLUTCHING THE BOOK.   MORE
RUN IN CALLING AND STRIKING.   THE
STRUGGLE BECOMES A WHIRLING BELLI-
GERENT DANCE.)*

VOICES :  The Lord strike you !
                The Lord strike you !

  Atheist !
             Devil-worshipper !
                      Heretic !

  Blasphemer !
            Traitor !
                  Schismatic !
                          Idolator !

Will you touch God's church ?
           Will you silence God's word ?

Here is Christ !
      here is Christ !
              here !
                here !

Therefore curse them !
      Give them great pain !

Hurt them !
      Kill them !
              Hang them !
                Burn them !

THE ACCUSER :  When Messias promised once that he would
                         dwell
within his Church for ever, you did not think
that this was all you would let him do for you ;
this the only way you would have him walk,

and his merciful talk twisted to terrible agonies.

CANTERBURY : Hark yet, brother ! I heard a voice
speaking, and another : God's choice is other than ours.
(*FROM THE HEAVENS THE FIGURES OF
THE LAST LORD ABBOT OF COLCHESTER
AND OF THE PROTESTANT MARTYR ROSE
ALLEN APPEAR. THEY COME A LITTLE
DOWN THE STEPS AND STAND. THE
DANCE PAUSES IN A RIGID TABLEAU.*)

THE ABBOT : I was Thomas Becke, Benedictine, abbot
of St. John Baptist at Colchester. Four hundred years
had passed since the Norman founded it before I
followed my centuries of predecessors to the chair.
There I looked to serve my Lord in quiet,
but bare presently stood our abbey against
King Henry's rages ; there came a flood of axes
that had cried havoc on many great glories
and made cells of holy contemplation cellars
for bats winged to other flights than heaven's.
The King called me to his new oaths, but I
was thralled by the old. I denied his will ; then
here they took me and hanged me by my own door.
I died—unworthy I—as many before
died for God's glory ; therefore by his will now—
O unworthy, unworthy !—I glow among the martyrs.

ROSE ALLEN : I was Rose Allen, a girl of Essex ;
few knew me then, and of you now none.
Fresh I ran with other younglings in the fields,
grew, and helped, I too, with the brewing and churning ;
till God spoke to me out of my heart
in a blessed simpleness ; grace woke,
and I—poor I—had to brace myself to the post.
The Holy Ghost would fare through me ; then
bare I stood, with my mother and my fellows, against

Queen Mary's rage ; there came a flood of fire
over the Essex flats ; there was I ;
on a day, on a day, I would not deny my Lord,
a cord was round my waist and laced tight
was I to the stake and the faggot—covered to the middle.
I burned—unworthy I—as many before
burned to God's glory ; therefore by his will now—
O unworthy, unworthy !—I glow among the martyrs.

THE ABBOT : Blessed Essex, be known in love for ever !
ROSE ALLEN : Blessed Essex, be known in love for ever !
THE ABBOT : Thus it was once, sister !
ROSE ALLEN :                     Brother, thus it was !

> (*THEY RUN DOWN AND ARE SWALLOWED IN THE CROWD.*)

VOICES : Down with those who preach the new gospel !
Down with those who keep the old canons !
Down with the abbots !
                    Down with the gospellers !

                                        Burn !

hang, torture, kill ? let none escape.
                    THE CHORUS.
He that does it to the least of these
for ever and ever does it to me :
It is I they hunt, it is I they seize,
it is I they slay—and I do not flee,
for it is my will always to bring
a good thing out of iniquity.

He that hates the least of these
for ever and ever has hated me :
much though he sorrow when he sees,
and be pardoned much, yet this must be—
that he hardened his heart against gentleness
he shall confess to eternity.

*(THE CROWD FALL BACK, SHOWING THE
BOUND FIGURES OF THE MARTYRS BACK
TO BACK.)*

CHELMSFORD : Did I do this ?

THE ACCUSER :            Those who were of you did.
  And wisely Augustine chid those who thought
  they were free from the sins of those who went
                        before them.

CHELMSFORD : O rid me—can any ? can Messias ?—of this
                              woe !

ST. CEDD : Nay, since this cannot change, know
  rather the range of his mercy.  Man is one
  in sin from beginning to end, nor otherwise within
  sin's consummation, sin's opposite, the work of Man's
                           Son,
  God's Son, Christ of the double Nature ; now
  he brings as ever from the worst hour a power
  bounteous with all good of all kind.

THE SEES : Be with us, be with us, be with us, to the end of
                          the world !

*(THEY STRETCH THEIR HANDS TOWARDS
THE MARTYRS.)*

THE ABBOT : Pater Noster

ROSE ALLEN : Our Father

THE ABBOT : qui es in coelis

ROSE ALLEN : which art in heaven

THE ABBOT : Panem nostrum quotidianum da nobis

ROSE ALLEN : give us this day our daily bread.

CANTERBURY : Their souls in death intercede with the one
                          Christ,
  and that heavenly breath hath sufficed ; the thing is
                          done.
  Christ hath won himself again out of the pit :
  go, one of you, release their souls to peace.

*(A SERAPH RUNS DOWN AND TOUCHES THE CORD; IT FALLS. THE MARTYRS TURN TO EACH OTHER.)*

Rose Allen : Brother, what you said was true in the Church :
see now, here are the Rites saved,
beyond me, beyond you, by your doing ; beyond both
saved through Christendom by true men's contrition.
I see I was not the only one with a mission,
though indeed mine was given me by your need.

The Abbot : Sister, what you did was great in the Church :
see now here is the Book saved,
graved in English words upon English hearts.
It shall blow as the wind of youth ; it shall take youth
with wonder, nor age lose it nor death deny.
The Word to wayfaring men shall testify
how his graces transubstantiate times and places,
nor shall any release from the claws of John's eagle
this land, till the poor find peace, and the rich goodwill,
and the course be one with its end.
Faith herein shall befriend for ever our folk,
hope, and the thing that is more than hope or faith.
Thus it saith for ever : O gift, O grafted power
in the power of men's souls : Christ singer, Christ voice,
Christ song.

Rose Allen : Hark, we are called back !

The Abbot : The spiral beauty
cries us again to the strain of its song : come.

*(THEY RE-ASCEND, WHILE THE SONG OF THE DIOCESE IS SUNG BY THE CROWD.)*

See now the Church of thy choosing, fair Spring of Salvation ;
design of the universe, hasten our hearts to thy using ;
incline into glory thy cherished and changing creation
till thy kingdom be come and we lift in a living oblation.

Wonder and Splendour, exhibit the truth of thy making ;
bidding us choose, thou hast sworn by thyself to be tender ;
ridding our evil away, thou hast met us, forsaking
all things but thee ; we are thine, O our Love, for the taking.

The death, that in thee was abiding, redeem us from dying,
we hiding in thee as in Manhood thy Godhead was hiding ;
guide through the Life that was fair from thy mother our
                                        sighing,
and close in the Church of thy choosing man's uttermost
                                        crying.

Thou wert the only beginning, O soon be the ending ;
we move, at thy thrust, to the joy that is ours for the
                                        winning ;
O Love that art victory, thine was the gracious expending ;
thou hast made us for thine, and thy heart is the full
                                        comprehending.


St. Cedd : Disperse, lords of heaven, the sorrowful shadows
        of those that wrought the woe ; disperse hate,
        folly, false love ; bid all be gone.
The Sees (as they speak, the crowd disperse unhappily) :
        O Lord, who hast taught us that all our doings without
        charity are nothing worth ; Send thy Holy Ghost, and
        pour into our hearts that most excellent gift of charity,
        the very bond of peace and of all virtues, without which
        whosoever liveth is counted dead before thee : Grant
        this for thine only Son Jesus Christ's sake. *Amen.*

ANTIOCH : Wise were you, brother, in what you showed,
 and well may all we take note of the action,
 the fraction of the Sacred Body : yet Christendom
 has caught the style of Christ ; brother, how ?
 Cedd, where have you seen him this long while ?

ST. CEDD : Men's fires were lit not only for destroying
 but fit to warm households, to help the enjoying
 of the commonness of life ; nay, perhaps the rage
 of prophets and patriarchs is no greater thing
 than in every age the mere stirring of goodwill.
 True that our Lord was God, but then Man too ;
 and he dined and drank wine and slept and wept and
       knew
 his mother and his friends : this is a sweet mystery
 how he could love all and yet love some
 after his flesh, therefore he laboured for flesh,
 and gave us lords and learners to help flesh.
 And blessed be he that they left here their names—
 as at Hempstead William Harvey who first found
 how the blood moves in the body, or at Upton
 Joseph Lister who purified hurts and stayed
 Death's creeping germs, and brought to be
 healing of many multitudes ; at Maldon and Witham
 Rayleigh who framed the constitution of the air,
 and named a new thing from its mere idleness—
 no wise idle he ; nor William Byrd
 who at Stondon, devising ' strange chromatic notes,
 compassionated his voice to the choice of music '.

CHELMSFORD : These were great masters, and worked secretly ;
    their doing lurked in the cells of their own brain.
    But rather bring now, lord, a wider thing to the viewing ;
    show ordinary lives, gay as gay they can be,
    no remonstrant distress or remarkable delight,
    but bright in their own tinctures of every day
    and descended from the blood of the great knight Adam
    when first he bore manfully his coat of arms
    through the desert and by grace won the wilderness with
                       charms.
    Adam are we all ; this is more than all degree.
ST. CEDD : To this therefore, see, we let grow the young
    in fullness of fragrance when the Faith from its own fate
    kept holiday in churches, in convents and schools,
    as on the feast of fools, of boy-bishops and girl-abbesses,
    nor least at your house of Barking ; there the maids
    by legal licence overturned law and saw
    the abbess deposed and her quiet closed in riot,
    when rudeness was shrived, and goodness of laughter
      thrived,
    and fathers and friends and all the world's folk
    came to the feast of the Triduum at Christmastide.
          (*THE GIRLS OF BARKING ABBEY ENTER,
          CHASING THE NUNS AND THEN BRINGING
          THE GIRL-ABBESS IN PROCESSION, TWO
          OR THREE NUNS, NICHOLAS UDALL AND
          ANOTHER PRIEST (THE CONVENT CON-
          FESSOR), AND A FEW OF THE GENTRY.*)
ONE OF THE GIRLS : Make way for the Lady Abbess
    Catherine !
ALL : Make way.
ONE OF THE GIRLS : High day keep we under own our abbess ;
    prioress and novice-mistress are put down
    and we govern them now as they year-long

rule us, poor creatures, with frown and bitter saying.
Now is our feast and all they plight to our playing.

(*SHE BREAKS OFF.*)

I am thirsty with making proclamations; Dame
Margaret, bring me a drink of milk.

THE GIRLS: Forfeit, forfeit! Anne, you called her Dame!

ANNE I......(she gives in) I did!

ANOTHER GIRL: Bring her to the Lady Abbess; she shall ask
pardon of all of us—

ANOTHER: And flat on her face, of the whole convent of us.
Get you down, Anne.

ANNE: I appeal to the Lady Catherine!

THE GIRL-ABBESS: I do not think she need go *flat*. Sister
Anne, you must kneel and ask pardon of me and the
whole blessed sisterhood for high scandal and offence
done against the time of the Triduum and our high
feast and the rule of your unworthy sister me, your
abbess, by calling the deposed mistress of the novices
Dame.

ANNE: It would be me, of course.

(*SHE KNEELS DOWN; THE GIRLS ARE
ROUND IN A CIRCLE.*)

Please you, my Lady Abbess, and you, my venerable
sisters, to pardon me for this wickedness: mea culpa,
mea culpa, mea culpa!

THE GIRL-ABBESS: We excuse you. (Anne rises.) And listen,
all of you. You know that our Reverence, having been
sick of a fever these three weeks, has seen nothing of your
play for Holy Innocents, and we are determined to mend
this piece of ill-luck. It is quite indecent that we should
be compelled to wait until every nun in the convent sees
it; so we will have it done before us now.

ONE OF THE YOUNGER NUNS: O come! Not another rehearsal!

> (*SHE STOPS SUDDENLY, CLAPPING HER HAND ON HER MOUTH.*)

THE GIRL-ABBESS (awfully): What did you say, Sister Felicitas?

THE NUN: Nothing, Lady Abbess.

THE GIRL-ABBESS: If I thought you were insubordinate—

THE NUN: Not at all, Lady Abbess.

THE GIRL-ABBESS: I would have you read aloud a homily of the blessed Saint Augustine instead, by yourself, where we could hear your voice and need not listen. Take care. Produce your company of wholesome actors.

THE NUN (meekly): Do you want *all* the play?

THE GIRL-ABBESS (glancing round): What does everyone think?

> (*THERE IS A GENERAL MURMUR WHICH SUGGESTS DEFINITE DISSENT.*)

Well, perhaps not *all*. A scene or so. Which is the most amusing? What about the Temptation of St. Mary?

THE NUN: That is very amusing.

THE GIRL-ABBESS: We will have that then. Who wrote the Play?

NICHOLAS UDALL: Your servant, Lady Abbess.

THE GIRL-ABBESS: What, you, Nicholas! We didn't see you. Is it a good play?

NICHOLAS UDALL: A very good play indeed, Lady Abbess.

ONE OF THE GIRLS: It is poetry, is it not?

UDALL: It is.

THE GIRL: Do you like writing poetry?

UDALL: It is rather difficult sometimes. One has to work extremely hard at it, even though I am one of the best poets in the kingdom.

THE GIRL-ABBESS (with interest) : Really ? I thought it all just......(she waves her hand vaguely) came. Did King David have to work when he wrote the psalms ? are they poetry ?

UDALL : They are, Lady Abbess, and he did. If anyone tells you that poetry comes (he waves his hand as she did), Lady Abbess, tell him—tell him he is an infidel and an unbeliever. Almighty God does not give those things as easily as all that.

THE GIRL-ABBESS : Really ? You astonish me, father. The Lady Abbess whose place Our Reverence has the honour of filling for a few hours always gave us to understand that that was the way in which she composed her hymns for the use of the convent. (She looks round). Shall we make them have a disputation about it ?

THE CONFESSOR (tactfully interrupting) : I think, Lady Abbess, it travels rather far into matters of theology ; it becomes almost a matter of the operation of the Holy and Blessed Spirit ; a matter reserved to His Holiness at Rome.

THE GIRL-ABBESS (a little disappointed) : Well, if you say so......

UDALL (supporting his colleague) : And what about the play ?

THE GIRLS : Yes, yes, the play.

THE GIRL-ABBESS : Yes, the play. Sister Felicitas, proceed. Stand you back, fathers, and you, gentlemen, and give them room.

THE GIRLS : Come on, come ! Where are the Seven Deadly Sins ? Mary—where's Mary ?

ALL : Mary ! Mary Magdalen !

THE PRODUCER (taking over) : Come, come, to your places, all of you ! Obey your Lady Abbess !

*(THE SEVEN SINS GO ON ONE SIDE ; MARY
AND THE GIRLS ON THE OTHER. WHILE
THEY DO SO, THE CONFESSOR TAKES THE
PRODUCER ASIDE.)*

THE CONFESSOR : It is a little late now and I don't want to
interfere, but I'm not happy about Mary Magdalen.
She's a good girl, of course, but she's young and a little
flighty. I wish you could have someone more devout.
Now there's Tabitha—I never quite knew why you made
Tabitha take the part of Sloth ; one of the quietest and
devoutest girls in the school. Why couldn't she have
been the Magdalen ?

THE PRODUCER : She's a worse actress, father. She does much
better as Sloth. Mary makes a finer show.

THE PRIEST : But she's not so pious.

THE PRODUCER : If piety can't act, Father, piety ought not
to be in a play. Our sweet Lord told us that piety ought
to be private, and devotion in the inner room. He said
nothing about it doing anything outside. Tabitha's only
got to look lumpish as Sloth, not—whatever Mary Magdalen looked. You must forgive me ; every one of us
to a proper job !

*(THE CONFESSOR RETIRES. THE PRODUCER
TURNS TO THE ACTORS.)*

Now, are you ready ? Away. (She claps her hands.)

MARY AND THE GIRLS : Dull it is in tide of spring
       to sit and hear the birds sing
       but never our eyes to be waking
         on any goodly show.

MARY : But see now by Bethany
       who may these bright gentles be,
       clothed in such gay livery ?
         'Fore heaven, I love them so.

| | |
|---|---|
| THE SINS (in procession) : | Clothes many have we to wear, jewels rich and head-gear fair ; come, you people all who care for a fresh day and a fine— |

THE PRODUCER : Now, now, for shame ! is a sin so dull ? come, tempt ! one would think none of you had ever sinned in your lives. Luxury, lavish yourself more ; and Anger, start and brandish your sword. You have all the rest of the year to repent in ; come now ! Only Sloth is to look as sleepy as she chooses.

THE CONFESSOR (as the Producer comes near him) : Do not be profane, sister ; we must not mock at holy things.

THE PRODUCER (indignantly) : Who is mocking at holy things, Father ? I am as good a Christian as yourself, and what these girls don't know about the sins I shall never be likely to teach them. To them, Mary !

| | |
|---|---|
| MARY : | Gentles, if it please you, say who ye are that walk so gay, and why ye go this way : we marvel how ye shine. |
| GLUTTONY : | Happy are they to me thralled : Gluttony am I called ; I have what I will to eat. |
| SLOTH : | But comfort much in peace have I who can hardly open an eye ; Sloth is my name and seat. |
| HATE : | I am a high lord in man's life, having in me all roots of strife, and Hate I have to name. |

ONE OF THE GENTRY : I don't understand that.

ANOTHER : No, nor do I. Ask her what it means.

THE FIRST GENTLEMAN (to the Producer) : Sister, what does that mean ?

THE PRODUCER (absently watching the Sins dance) : What does what mean, Sir ?

THE SECOND GENTLEMAN : What Hate says—about roots of strife.

THE PRODUCER : I can't explain now : ask Father Nicholas— he wrote it.

THE FIRST GENTLEMAN (to Udall) : Hi, you, Nicholas man, what do you mean by what Hate says ?

UDALL : That ?  O well, my lord...that...that...that means... Well (he talks very quickly) my lord, that means that Hate is one of those sins which have most power over men, out of which spring all the worst kinds of evil, as cruelty, buffetings, quarrellings, angers, bloodsheds, affrays, slanderings, and the rest, for all these have indeed their beginnings and fertile growths in that hatred which is engendered between one man and another, and so this hatred is a lord, as one might say, Dominus, but the short word is the better here, and so he calls himself, and takes pride in it, which is indeed the very root mark of all sin, for it is its nature to be delighted with itself and not with another, as all love's true disciples be.

THE PRODUCER : Sh'h !

UDALL : Do you see now, my lord ?

THE FIRST GENTLEMAN : A very difficult way of saying a very simple thing.

UDALL (aside) : Go and hunt rats with Beelzebub.

MARY AND THE GIRLS :   Hear you, girls, how they say ?
                         Methinks to go with them away
                         were a good roundelay
                         on a morn of spring.

ANGER :   Anger am I, a lofty lord ;
                         with any who dare my sharp sword
                         I have a bold reckoning.

| | |
|---|---|
| ENVY : | Envy's dress has colour quiet<br>but rich as any in this riot,<br>    and her venom sharper than<br>        steel. |
| PRIDE : | I am Pride ; I need no stuff<br>rich or fair ; it is enough<br>    for me never to kneel. |

THE SECOND GENTLEMAN : And why should Envy have a sad-coloured dress, I should like to know ? Why, the plays they give at Court are not as difficult as this, and there all the learned men of Europe come. But they dance prettily enough.

> (*HE CATCHES HOLD OF ENVY AS SHE PASSES HIM, INTERRUPTING THE REHEARSAL.*)

Do you understand that, my girl ?

ENVY (curtseying and impertinent) : Of course, father.

THE FIRST GENTLEMAN : Why your dress is to be so sober, hey ?

ENVY : Of course. It's as simple as the Holy Gospel.

THE SECOND GENTLEMAN : Ha, indeed. Is the Gospel simple, Nicholas ?

UDALL : Well—in a way, yes, sir.

THE CONFESSOR (in an undertone) : Brother, the Gospel is not simple, and you know it.

UDALL : Well—in a way, no, brother.

THE GIRL-ABBESS : My lords, we are waiting for the rehearsal to proceed. We are to remind you that you are here only by our courtesy and our invitation. Release Sister Envy and pray stand back.

THE SECOND GENTLEMAN : Baggages, aren't they ? (He cuffs Envy lightly back to her place.) Get away with you, daughter. (To his friend.) The money they cost us and the airs they put on.

THE PRODUCER : Now, Luxury !

LUXURY :  I am sovereign of this whole cartel,
   ruler of the pits of hell,
   but the world is mine as well :
    will you not walk with me ?
   I am pleasant and satisfying
   to all men's easy lying.
    I am called Luxury.

THE SINS (to the Girls) : Ah, flowers of sweet worth,
   will you not come and have great mirth
    with us in our house ?

LUXURY (to Mary) : But you are the fairest of them all ;
   we will have each other, whate'er befall,
    by everlasting vows.

  *(THE GIRLS PAIR OFF WITH THE SINS.)*

THE FIRST GIRL (to Gluttony) : Ever I had a sweet tooth,

THE SECOND GIRL (to Sloth) : and I loved slumber well for-
sooth.

THE THIRD GIRL (to Hate) : Dove's eyes have you, my dear ;

THE FOURTH GIRL (to Pride) : I in your arms be without fear.

THE FIFTH GIRL (to Anger) : Sweetly, fair lord, you frighten
me.

THE SIXTH GIRL (to Envy) : Cover me well, sweet Envy.

MARY MAGDALENE : Cover me well, and I will abide,
 noble Luxury, by thy side
  for ever and a day ;
 Unless there come a king so dread
 that he could harry the very dead
  shall none draw me away.

THE PRODUCER : O passion, passion ! My good girl, you are
Mary Magdalen giving yourself up to sensuality. For
heaven's sake ! Our fair lady Magdalen was no coy
cloisterer of sin ; whatever she did I warrant she did it
with an air, even if she only wore red gloves. Come,

come ! you are defying the whole world ! Yes, and more, for now you are plighting yourself to the Lord who is to come, and you do not know it ! Heartbreak, heartbreak ! Come, again.

MARY (as before) : Cover me well, and I will abide,
noble Luxury, by thy side
for ever and a day ;
Unless there come a king so dread
that he could harry the very dead
shall none draw me away.

THE PRODUCER : Now, all of you, clap and carol.

(*THE DANCE OF THE GIRLS AND THE SINS, THE SPECTATORS ACCOMPANYING.*)

THE CONFESSOR (to the Girl-Abbess) : It is almost time for Compline.

THE GIRL-ABBESS : It is very good, isn't it ? We thank you, sisters. You will come with us now to the chapel where we shall enthrone ourselves in the Lady Abbess's chair and listen to Compline. Let us proceed in peace.

ALL THE GIRLS (ranging themselves in a sudden change to a real beauty of devotion) : In the name of Jesus.

(*THEY FILE OUT. THE PRODUCER STOPS UDALL.*)

THE PRODUCER : O Father, may I speak to you ? Look, we really need some of St. John's speeches cut, and two more written in for the tormentors ; and we ought to have something funnier for the Court of the Emperor— it's rather dull as it stands. O and the Archangel Gabriel says that the names of the devils are hard to remember, and could you find her some easier ones ? Where did you get these from ?

UDALL : From a learned Jew in London : they are the real thing.

THE PRODUCER : They may be but I think we should have
    Christian devils.  The Lady Abbess will like it better.  It
    is no use having learned devils—plain simple Satan is
    enough for her.
UDALL (as they go out) :  Much too much for all of us, my
    sister.
THE ACCUSER :  Beautiful are the mild moments ; fair and fit
    are feasts and fasts in the seasons' flight ; wit
    flashes to heaven more from a full stomach
    than ever from an empty, save only where
    those who are called to it climb the steep stair
    of convents or rigour of rules : else—
    forget you, gentles, the tale the Gospel tells ?
    Messias came eating and drinking ; men said,
    *behold a gluttonous man and a winebibber*.  Cedd,
    what did he leave for his folk ?
ST. CEDD :                             Flesh and blood,
    meat and drink for the heart's grace.
THE ACCUSER :                          Good.
    Why now does the Church outface his blessing ?
    Where is the meat and drink meant for the poor ?
ST. CEDD : What do you mean, brother ? what word
    of scandal against us tingles now on your tongue ?
THE ACCUSER : Scandal ? Judge ! I accuse the Church thus—
    I accuse her that always and everywhere—now and here—
    she has been comatose to man's earthly need ;
    I accuse her that she has given no heed to the poor,
    that she has allowed kings and rich men
    to be masters of the poor and of herself, and a den
    full only of foulness left for the dispossessed ;
    I accuse her of offering heaven as an excuse for horror,
    of the abuse of Christ's flesh and blood ; more—
    I accuse her therefore of making schism in the unity
    of flesh and spirit, of spoiling the seamless robe ;

more—of heresy and thrice heresy,
of foiling the Single Person, God and Man,
by abusing the flesh that is his in the forms of others
and digging God's grave in the gaunt bodies of his

brothers.

Answer if you can—

ROME :                                              No slow answer ;
I may speak for all the West, for little rest
have the preachers in a thousand years had from

declaring

it is ill faring for the Faith and small comfort
when the rulers of realms leave the poor to grieve ;
parish priests and princes of the paparchy bear
witness against this tyranny everywhere.

THE ACCUSER : Is it so ? make answer then—not to me !

not to me !

Be your answer to the people ! ah, do you shake ?
What have you done when the people began to wake ?
did you not make a refuge of the ark of salvation
when the hail peltered and the flood rose ?  Hark !

(HE CALLS DOWN.)

God and the people, speak ! speak, you
who by the body of his passion are his true kin !

*(A NUMBER OF MEN AND WOMEN BEGIN TO ENTER.)*

THE CHORUS : All these years we have heard from heaven
the prayer that out of his mouth was given :
*Give us this day our daily bread.*
We have heard priests and preachers teach
young children to say in their small speech :
*Give us this day our daily bread.*
Cakes of offal and beds of straw
are easier to give than an equal law :
*Give us this day our daily bread.*
What when the poor begin to take
hold on the laws that their masters make ?
*Give us this day our daily bread.*
Then the lords begin to pray,
then the lawyers hastily say :
*Give us this day our daily bread.*
And lest they should call on Messias in vain,
they seize it before they pray again :
*Give us this day our daily bread.*

*(A CROWD OF POOR PEOPLE HAVE GATHERED. A PRIEST ENTERS.)*

THE FIRST MAN : Father, must we pay tax when we need bread ?

A WOMAN : Bread, father !

ANOTHER WOMAN : Father, bread.

THE SECOND MAN : I heard an abbot once, preaching in his
                                    abbey
    say a man had a right to his meed of food :
    having none, if he took it, he were no thief !

THE FIRST MAN : Nay, I heard the Bishop of Rochester say
    the King owed all his liegemen relief
    from their burdens ; why then should we pay tax ?

A WOMAN : Father, food is scant ; we want succour.

THE PRIEST : Alas, children, I have no more than you.
    I cannot help it ; I have lived long among you
    and you know I have never thrived when you needed
    nor wassailed when you wanted.  My lords are away
    in great towns, busy with much trouble
    of foreign crowns and lands, politics and the like.

A MAN : Does the King himself know the pains of his people ?

A WOMAN : Has the King blood in his veins ? does he
    sleep ?

THE PRIEST : Alas, the King is young and deep in business,
    consulting with the Emperor and many great dukes,
    propounding the boundaries of the Turk beyond Danube
    perhaps, or how to save Constantinople.
    Be patient, children.

THE WOMAN : We have been patient since the world began,
    Let them leave the Danube and save us,
    as they could have saved my man who died in the
                                    famine,
    gnawing a few leaves.  I lay all night
    saying what they said God wills us to say :
    *Give us this day our daily bread.*  He is dead.
    Where was his bread ? did the King or the armed lords
    or the merchants or the lawyers or the fat furred
                                    foreigners

who ride so fast down the roads to London help?
Father, if God meant to us to live decently
there is knavery in the air; his goodness is stolen
                                somewhere.

THE PRIEST: Be patient and mild, daughter. God sends
tribulation as a means of testing his friends;
no resting if no running; trust,
trust him to give you back more than you lost,
and a purchase so great that the payment is little cost.

A MAN: Empty bellies are bad believers;
give us a crust or two; we shall trust better.
        *(ENTER ANOTHER PRIEST.)*

THE SECOND PRIEST: Essex is up! they have met at Brent-
                              wood all.

Thomas the baker at Fobbing refused the taxes,
and my lord Chief Justice who had come down with
                              commissions
has galloped back to London; we missed *him*
but the heads of his clerks hurry after him on poles.
        *(CHEERING.)*

Kent is up too. Wat Tyler leads,
Essex-born, though has lived in Kent long,
We met his fellows at Barking. Up, all!

THE FIRST PRIEST: Folly!

THE SECOND PRIEST: No, folly. We have a fine watchword:
" Who holds with King Richard and the true commons? "
Who of you are true men?

THE CROWD: All! all!
God save King Richard and the true commons!
        *(ANOTHER MAN RUNS IN.)*

THE MAN: Ho, news for Everyman! a message for Everyman!
Thus says John Ball the preacher:
John Sheep-herd, priest of Colchester, greets well John

Nameless and John the Miller, and John Carter, and bids
them be ware of guilefulness in the towns; and bids them
stand together in God his name, and bids Piers Plough-
man go to his work, and chastise well Hob the Robber;
and take with you John Trueman and all his fellows and
none other, and have you one head and no more.

John Miller, John Carter, John Trueman, John
                              Nameless,
all true Johns, all true Nameless,
come to the King!

SHOUTS: All the Nameless to the King!

> *MORE MEN THRONG IN. JOHN BALL
> ENTERS. THERE IS LOUD CHEERING.)*

JOHN BALL: Hear, men and women! To be poor,
when all are poor, is a trick of the bad weather;
or to have, when all honest folk stand together,
some a little richer, some a little poorer,
must be as may be; God's clay are all,
and Christ send his Christmas merrily to all.
But now is a new thing which is very old—
that the rich make themselves richer and not poorer,
which is the true Gospel, for the poor's sake.
Do you know what Holy Church says? Holy Church
says when you need food you have a right to take it,
and no sin; it is within her law
that no man has any right to rob his brother,
and a man may use arms to preserve his own.
Many bishops and learned clerks say
this is God's truth: I tell you what Holy Church
teaches; now is the time we followed the teaching—
to the King! to the King! down with false clerics!
down with all lawyers! the King of England
shall save the English yet: nameless men,

come you all to the bounty of God and the King.
This is how we know the Kingdom of God,
that the rich make themselves poorer and not richer.
It is our business to see that his kingdom comes—
quickly.

(*CHEERING.*)

No man who is not in grace can own property ;
he has no place in God's household, no right,
be his might or his rank what they may, to be steward
of Christ's furnishings for Christ's folk : say,
can churls and cheats be chosen for God's stand-bys ?
churls though lords, cheats because lawyers ?  I,
John Ball, John Nameless, tell you all,
and will tell the King or the Pope in Rome to his face,
no man not in grace can own property ;
through all creation salvation is the root of dominion ;
title-deeds are nothing unless the Lamb signs them ;
they damn a man deeper.  Who dare deny—
who ?—that the devil can only own the devil,
and the devil's children can possess nothing but
                                    themselves.
Therefore up, follow to London ! swear—
and you shall see the foreigners flee before you—
to be faithful to God and the King and the true
                                    Commons !
ALL : God and the King and the true Commons !  On.

(*THEY  POUR  OUT.*)

THE CHORUS : Babylon now sits quiet on Tiber and Thames,
    sleepy with drunkenness ; over her the many jewels
    are little licking flames confined in beauty ;
    the scarlet of martyrs' blood stains her purple
    and drains down to the sound of instruments of music.
    Count the kinds of merchandise she buys—

VARIOUS VOICES : Gold
                    silver
                            precious stones
                                        silks
            scents
                    ointments
                            frankincense
                                    cinnamon
                                        oil.
            All manners of vessels of iron
                                brass
                                    marble
            wood
                    ivory.
                            All manner of food
            fine flour
                    wheat
                            wines.
                                    All manner of riches
            bulls
                    sheep
                            horses
                                    dogs
                                        cars
            ships
                    trumpets
                            music
                                    great arts
                cities
                        slaves
                            women
                                and souls of men.
THE CHORUS :
    Alas, alas, that great city London !

The merchants of earth shall weep and mourn over her,
for no man shall buy their merchandise any more ;
there shall be no eyes to see or hands to finger
or ears to linger at all for sweet sounds :
deaf and blind and half-paralytic
she shall stumble into the judgement away from God,
to feed evermore on the chaff she proffered the poor.

CHELMSFORD : I have said it ! I have kept the faith ! Cedd,
witness that no year has gone by
that somewhere—at Thaxted or else—I have not cried
that the people must be saved in earth as in Heaven
and the angels dash pride into the pit.

ST. CEDD : It is so ; since God let his heavenly wit
dwell on earth, hell has never quite
battened the hatches down to make all tight
and the sentries set where its ship floats on the sea.
Hell has met always with windy weather.

THE ACCUSER : I do not deny it ; but let the commons try
to put into action what the common doctrine says
and back they are driven down the old ways
by the wall of gold, iron and steel. See—
it is not altogether your fault, sister, I agree.
Man finds the doctrine of exchange hard and strange—
see how your rebels fared once with King Richard.

       (*SOME OF THE REBELS ARE DRIVEN IN BY
       A WALL OF ARMED MEN, ALL IN STEEL
       WITH FACES COVERED BY STEEL. THEY
       MOVE LIKE AUTOMATA.  THE REBELS
       ARE SCATTERED OR SLAIN OR TAKEN.*)

THE CAPTAIN OF THE ARMED MEN (in a booming metallic
                     voice) :
Take the chief of the rebels to execution.
It is good that a few men should die for the State.

THE ACCUSER : He is right, is he ? or is he not ? God
   ignored the argument ; he merely died.

> *(THE ARMED MEN MOVE OUT, CONVEYING*
> *THE REBELS.)*

CHELMSFORD : With each childbirth the struggle begins again ;
   no sooner have a few men known their sins
   than they die, and the old easy grudge stirs
   in the hearts of the new age ; it prefers
   bestiality of pomp to the peace of blessing.
   How long, O Master of heaven ?  Lord, how long ?

THE ACCUSER : I do not say your are wrong, sister ; your task
   is hard.  Heaven may ask for impossibilities,
   but it rarely gets them.  That perhaps is as much
   its own fault as yours ; I may say so—but you,
   rue and repent : that is what you have to do.

ANTIOCH : Nor you alone, little sister ; all we
   lament for the quailing and the failing.  Here
   in heaven repentance itself is a wonderful laughter,
   a beauty of God's devising ; but recall we now,
   lords and brothers, the bitter moments below
   when we knew how we went the way we would not go.

> *(ALL THE SEES AND CHELMSFORD KNEEL.)*

ALL THE SEES AND CHELMSFORD :
   Have mercy upon me, O God, after thy great goodness :
   according to the multitude of thy mercies do away mine
   offences.
   Wash me thoroughly from my wickedness : and cleanse
   me from my sin.
   For I acknowledge my faults : and my sin is ever before
   me.
   Against thee only have I sinned, and done this evil in
   thy sight : that thou mightest be justified in thy saying,
   and clear when thou art judged.

Behold, I was shapen in wickedness : and in sin hath my
mother conceived me.

But lo, thou requirest truth in the inward parts : and
shalt make me to understand wisdom secretly.

Thou shalt purge me with hyssop, and I shall be clean :
thou shalt wash me, and I shall be whiter than snow.

Thou shalt make me hear of joy and gladness : that the
bones which thou hast broken may rejoice.

Turn thy face from my sins : and put out all my mis-
deeds.

Make me a clean heart, O God : and renew a right spirit
within me.

Cast me not away from thy presence : and take not thy
holy Spirit from me.

O give me the comfort of thy help again : and 'stablish
me with thy free Spirit.

St. Cedd : And the blessing of the Mercy be on you all.

(*THE SEES RISE.*)

It is always the same and yet it is not the same.
Brothers, the Faith has done something, since
first our great Prince allied himself
to men on the side of their right instincts.  Much
is tattered and torn ; and long forlorn
amid barbarous angers and desires may men be,
as when from the sea came plunging the Danish fires
on Catholic Christendom, but he always there
ran up and down the stair of heaven.  See,
this is how it all went out, and how still
it may go out again, if the shout of the pirate crews
bursts from the cold clustered woods—the moods
and melancholy hungers of men are always piratical.
Call Osyth, my lords : did she die when she died ?
Her instinct was Christ's and deeper than theirs,
since she knew, as we know, that Love can love and
                                        be loved.
What else but the Faith has shown that truth to be
                                        true ?

THE CHORUS : Osyth, Osyth, Osyth !
Show from beatitude ! appear out of grace !
show again the time and the place
when the axe was the sign of the high heart's
                                        warmest embrace.
Blessed one, show !

*(CELESTIAL MUSIC. THE NUNS AND ST. OSYTH ENTER FROM HEAVEN. THEY DESCEND TO THE LOWER STAGE, AND GROUP THEMSELVES.)*

ST. OSYTH : Daughter and wife was I amid the East Saxons ;
    God called me at last to a third vocation—
    to a separation from all for his name's sake :
    blessedly my husband permitted it ; because he fitted
    his heart to my peace he shall never cease to know
    the goodness of God's will. I took the vows
    with God's authority and my husband's, presently I
                        ruled
    a house of nuns peaceably here in Essex,
    where we went about the business of understanding
    after our proper manner the expanding circles of Love.
    Remained that he deigned me yet a fourth
                        calling,
    installing me in a martyrdom—holy and happy is he.
    I left father for husband, husband for grace,
    grace for himself : the Danes took the islands
    on the Essex shore, and began from those forts to pour
    over the land, killing for pleasure, their leisure
    filled with savage torments. Christ be merciful
    to them and to us and to all ; Christ befall
    now and ever all men and all men's neighbours.

THE DANES (without) : Harou ! harou !
        *(THEY COME IN.)*

ST. CEDD : These are the two great instincts of man ;
    that is his state to be for ever torn
    between love and hate of love. Look, brother,
    our Lord took flesh to save the one from the other.
    Is it a wonder that some years must pass
    before wholly the dust of sin is changed
    to the manner of holiness everywhere ?

THE ACCUSER :                                   God made me just.
   I have admitted that he and you both
   have a hard labour in man's slow-witted heart.
   I can praise Osyth as well as you all.

        (*HE CALLS DOWN.*)

   Now, Osyth, now—for the vow and the veiling !

        (*THE FLIGHT AND MASSACRE OF THE
        NUNS.  OSYTH IS TAKEN.  SHE IS SET
        KNEELING AMONG THE DANES.*)

THE DANES (gathering round) : Harou ! harou !
ST. OSYTH : What shall I say ? am I to say that Love
   does not love and cannot be loved ?
THE DANES :                                   Harou !
THE DANISH CHIEFTAIN (holding his axe over her) :
   Say the axe is the only certain thing !
   Say the axe is your father and husband ; say
   the axe and the blood on the axe is your only lover.
   Say the blood on the axe is your only love !
ST. OSYTH : The blood on the cross is come again to its living :
   Love has no loss anywhere at all.
THE CHIEFTAIN : Harou !

        (*HE SWINGS THE AXE DOWN CLOSE TO HER
        HEAD.*)

   Say you are frightened of this axe.
ST. OSYTH :                             Of course I am frightened
   as I used first to be as a child when it lightened—
   but I laughed too ! as I laugh now at this,
   and at you, friend, if you will not think it unkind.
THE CHIEFTAIN : Feel the wind of Odin, and the Ravens
                                                flying !

        (*HE SWINGS THE AXE ON HER OTHER
        SIDE.*)

St. Osyth : I have felt a winter frost much colder,
   when I knelt before the altar of Love that loves.

The Chieftain : Say the axe is your father and mother and
                                          husband.

St. Osyth : I will attend to it rather, if my Lord wishes,
   for a sweet friend and task, as a cook to his dishes,
   an actor to his part, or the heart of man to his pleasant
   loves, till the present Christ take them all.
   Now is his name.

St. Cedd : His name is Now.

All the heavenly Persons : Now !

                *(THE DANES STRIKE OSYTH DOWN.)*

The Danes : Harou !

The Chief : Ravens, what temples stand against Odin ?
   death out of the sea takes them ;
   and the sea pours over and breaks them,
   and the Ravens hover above the cities ;
   they peck the eyes of the Romans flying,
   the falling consuls, the lictors dying ;
   Harou, harou, the Ravens hover.
   Rome is over the pit of the falling,
   Odin, send us the Ravens calling ;
   the axe is man's father and sister and brother,
   the blood on the axe is the mother of men.

The Danes : The axe !

                *(THE DANES POUR OUT.)*

The Chorus : Osyth, Osyth, Osyth !
   rise to beatitude ; take again place
   in the Glory apparent ; show how the Grace
   lifts to the life : blessed one, show !

                *(OSYTH HALF-RISES.)*

Chelmsford : No ; delay......
   What did you see, Osyth, as you died ?

ST. OSYTH : I saw the City where Love loves and is loved.
It was striking out of earth ; all the liking
of man for man, woman for woman, man for woman
opened outward into a glory ; it ran
out of the hidden points of the flesh and the soul
into the whole pattern of exchange of beauty,
and Fate free, and all luck good.

CHELMSFORD : How then ?

ST. OSYTH :                                   For all men
are man in him, and his two natures gather
all loves of all creatures to the love of the Father.

CHELMSFORD : Do not go, Osyth ; heaven is in you ;
you do not lack heaven, wherever you are.
Do not go back ; stay with me a little here.

ST. OSYTH : I were well willing to do this, if our Lord chose.

CHELMSFORD : Would he not ? entreat him for me : Patriarchs,
entreat him for me—
that Osyth and the blessed dead may tread my roads,
as at Bishop's Stortford and by Good and High Easter,
more perhaps at Pleshey where still
the bells ring triune to the enclosure of prayer.

JERUSALEM :                                   Nay, never
has our courteous Lord forbidden any to tread
earth, if her will be so : the blessed dead
are free everywhere through all the City—

THE ACCUSER : And indeed I am he who shows them to you.
I talk with them often by Brentwood and Dagenham,
down by Tilbury or away by Dunmow and the Baddows
and many places else on many evenings.
The more you know me, sweet, the more you know them.

CHELMSFORD : I begin to believe it, my lord ; only smile,
when you are harsh—and be as harsh as you will.
I shall believe in love the whole while.
I am a little afraid still—

THE ACCUSER:                                                          Princess,
    your eyes are as lovely in penitence as were the
                                                             Magdalene's.
JERUSALEM: Let Osyth do her will; she is in the Unity.
ST. OSYTH: I will go at once; I will find my old homes
    and many others—how, brother, did you name them?
    Brentwood, Dagenham, Tilbury, Dunmow, the Baddows.
    O sweet! I will go, I will go quickly.

> ((*SHE RUNS OUT.  CHELMSFORD BEGINS
> TO CRY FROM SHEER RELIEF.  THE AC-
> CUSER PASSES BEHIND HER AND SPEAKS,
> WITHOUT HER KNOWING CERTAINLY WHO
> IT IS.*)

THE ACCUSER: A little, a little; wait a little, sweet.

THE CHORUS :
    Messias that made man
    wishing him extravagance of love and great generosity
    began with as much of his own delight
    as ever to hold in his heart that figure had might.

    He began with himself for a plan :
    he formed an image of his joy and called it man ;
    he breathed therein everlasting desire for the bright
    clear intellectual vision of his own delight ;
    he sealed in the pure field of that lesser nature
    this that for ever he had in common with his creature.
    Man with man, woman with woman, man with woman,
    knows the lovely extravagance of joy,
    and, haste though they have and wild though it run to
                           waste,
    since Eve's hand thrust through the torn leaves,
    there is no other end in any his plight,
    in hell that deceives or heaven that justifies,
    than the candid wise vision of continual delight.
    He that is bone in man's bone and blood in man's blood,
    he that alone in the desert and sorrowful stood,
    he is feast in the feast and song in the song,
    strong in exercise, long in the laughter,
    maker of sensation, master of neighbourhood,
    mayor of the City of the Good in the blood and the bone.
CONSTANTINOPLE : Daughter, this is common knowledge
    in the low degrees of the heavenly college :

even in your world, even made with heavy hands,
the image of the joyous City stands.
What, since your time began, holds this in common?

CHELMSFORD : Man with man, woman with woman, man with
woman ;
God's grace has kept those joys in me, and I
witness before all devils that man's heart
is still more Christian than his wrangling will ;
legends and tales, and now to sound and sight
truth in our awful wonder of delight.

THE ACCUSER : Be humble, sweet ; delight is apt to lead
into bleak tombs of the spiritual dead.

CHELMSFORD : Cannot bones live ? what charnel place was left
uncleft when he ascended out of hell ?
Tell, songs of feasting ! love of woman, tell !

(*THE MUSIC OF OLD KING COLE*.)

THE CHORUS : Old King Cole and he called for his bowl
and he called for his fiddlers three,
and there was fiddle, fiddle, fiddle, and
—twice fiddle fiddle,
for 'twas my Lady's birthday,
and therefore keep we holiday
and a merry merry merry day.

(*KING COLE OF COLCHESTER ENTERS, WITH
HIS ATTENDANTS. WINE IS POURED OUT*.)

KING COLE : Blessed be peace now (they drink), and you,
my men,
betake yourselves well to drink's happiness, and the
harp's ;
these things flank fellowship.  Sit all down,
make good cheer and be jolly ; harvest
is in the barns, and the Twin Stars kind.
The Roman peace builds the barns, and the British
wheat fills it.  Picts and pirates lose

their hold on the land : go we now cheerfully
about our business in quiet.  Sit all down
and break voices in singing.  Who begins ?

THE FIRST MAN : Marcus, begin.

THE SECOND MAN : What shall I begin ?

KING COLE : What ?
  ' Bald-headed Caesar '—what else ?  Chorus, all.

The Song.

  Bald-headed Caesar went to Britain
  to sell his father's cast-off shoes :

*Chorus.* Wow, wow, wow and a fig for their fighting ;
  Colchester cackled and could not choose.
  Down the dirt ways, lump and thump,
  the by-blows of bald-headed Caesar stump.

  Hook-nosed Caesar went to Egypt
  to find a girl of Ptolemy's kind ;

*Chorus.* Wow, wow, wow and a fig for their flirting ;
  back he brought her and had to be blind.
  Down the dirt ways, lump and thump,
  the by-blows of hook-nosed Caesar stump.

  Bald-headed Caesar went to the Senate ;
  there the rich men stuck him with knives :

*Chorus.* Wow, wow, wow and a fig for their fumbling ;
  Caesar had more than a dozen lives.
  Down the dirt ways, lump and thump,
  the by-blows of bald headed Caesar stump.

  (*LOUD CHEERING. THEY ALL DRINK.*)

KING COLE (pouring out the libation) :
  To the Fortune of the Divine Emperor.

ALL (shouting and pouring) :
  To the Fortune of the Divine Emperor.

THE FIRST MAN : They say the Fortune of the Divine
             Emperor

may make him divine long before he wishes.
He has pains in his inside.

ALL : Sacrilege ! sacrilege !

THE SECOND MAN : The Sacred Emperor has no inside.

THE THIRD MAN : Or if he has, he has no pains there.

THE SECOND MAN : Or if he has, they are growing pains.—

Who
said once, when he felt death on him,
' I think I am on the point of becoming a god ' ?

KING COLE : Hush, fellows : you may talk so here,
but when you are in Rome—do as the Romans do.

THE FIRST MAN : Our lord and god Diocletian has an eye on
them.

THE SECOND MAN : He has held the Empire together ; he and
his Caesars.

THE THIRD MAN : And our own Constantius Chlorus not
least.

KING COLE : Some of you were with him in—

(A MESSENGER RUNS IN.)

THE MESSENGER : Sir, the excellent Caesar Constantius is
here.

KING COLE : What ?

THE MESSENGER : He has just ridden through the gates.
He has left the legions to march north ; himself
ridden here. In a moment he will be in the house.

KING COLE : Let us show well to Caesar.

(THEY PUT ON BEHAVIOUR. TRUMPETS.
CONSTANTIUS ENTERS, WITH THE EAGLES
AND A FEW OFFICERS. THE FORMAL
RECEPTION IN SILENCE.)

CONSTANTIUS CHLORUS :

We are very glad to know you, sir. Your town
has been a security to us now some years,
in a time when our legions have had sweaty work

on our frontiers, and within them sometimes.  Sir,
we are Rome ; it is Rome who thanks you now in us,
and do not think because you hear occasionally
of losses, defeats, massacres even, that Rome
is lost easily, for all the lavish raids
of the barbarians.  Sir, the Empire—
say rather the City, it is the greater name—
is more than all the noisy peoples, the races
shouting against each other from Persia to the Wall.
Tribal and national warcries sound everywhere
but Rome is settled beyond all nations and tribes.
If it went down—luck rules all—
you would have with some trouble to invent it again.
He is a wise nationalist who knows that his nation
is only half the truth ; the other half
he can only find by getting outside his nation.
That, sir, is the use of the City ; there
all the nations can know themselves through others ;
these must do so ; you, sir, know
that unless you live in the love of your neighbours you
                                            are nothing
but a silly noise, however loud.  So the peoples—
your British, for example—must learn to obey
Europe, Rome, the City.

KING COLE :                            My lord,
    because the City is beyond all tribes
    and all lives, even our dukedom of Colchester,
    I have believed in it and kept my people
    as a street in the City rather than a village of their own.
    I have been called disloyal and unpatriotic,
    no Briton ; better, they say, to run
    tribally howling, as free as the wolves in the woods,
    than to be only a gate to the great City.
    I have not thought so.

CONSTANTIUS : No.  If Rome lacks anything
   it is a soul worthy her ; a dream, a myth,
   a wonder of vision as much mightier than she
   as she than all the screaming animals of the races.
   The gods are old and tired ; only the sublime
   providence of our lord Diocletian sustains all things.
   The City, and a little friendship within the City—
   that is man's total sum of good.
   You can rest us here to-night ?
KING COLE :                              Sir, willingly.
   It may please your Highness that I present my child,
   my only one, a daughter, and a loyal friend of Rome.
CONSTANTIUS :  We are debtors everywhere to all such ; call
                                 her.
   And hark, privately a moment.

      (*SEVERAL GO OUT.  CONSTANTIUS AND
      THE KING COME DOWN TOGETHER.*)

                         Because you are a friend
   I will say this—do not answer me—if there be
   any of a sect called Christians among you,
   bid them not show while we are here.
   The divinity of the Emperor will have them cut off :
   that is one thing in Italy, but here quite another.
   I cannot afford the men to kill or be killed
   because of godheads.  Besides…but leave it there.
   I have had one man executed at Verulam
   who put himself in the way of it.  No more ; pass.

      (*HE TURNS AND SEES HELENA ENTERING.
      HE STANDS QUITE STILL.*)

KING COLE : I present, sir, my daughter and your Highness'
                                 servant.

      (*THEY STARE AT EACH OTHER.  HELENA
      GENUFLECTS.*)

CONSTANTIUS (mechanically) : We are very glad to see you.

HELENA (genuflecting again) : Sir and my lord.

CONSTANTIUS : I did not know that I was looking for
                                 anything......

KING COLE : My lord ?

CONSTNATIUS : ......and now suddenly I have found it.  Sir,
    to let the princess wear such jewels in her hair
    is to be reckless of riches.

KING COLE :                     My daughter wears
    no jewels, sir.

CONSTANTIUS : I did not think so, and yet
    I would not believe that her forehead was so bright.
    'Tis, yourself, sir, gives us permission.  You, gentlemen,
    leave us.

*(ALL BUT HELENA GO OUT.)*

                  It seems that I am still somebody ;
    a world or two moves when I speak, but I do not know
    why that should be.  Who are you ?

HELENA :                     Sir, my father
    told you : I am Helena of Colchester.

CONSTANTIUS :                     I
    was Constantius Chlorus the western Caesar ; now
    I am only the perception in a flash of love—

HELENA : A peremptory phenomenon of love,
    fiercer than your eagles.

CONSTANTIUS :                 All my eagles together
    have never frightened the Picts so much as I
    am frightened by the mere eyes of you.
    Is Love the only untired god that is left ?
    Do you believe, augustitude, in the gods ?
    It does not matter, only—we must say something
    lest we should go away or they come back.
    Speak to me then.

HELENA : Sir, I have been taught
that God is love and have heartily believed it,
but now I know that when our Lord took flesh
he made flesh so lordly that no God of Rome
was ever divinitized into such a glory.

CONSTANTIUS : Helena !

HELENA : Caesar !

CONSTANTIUS : I am Caesar again, now
you have given me back my function in the City.
What did you mean by what you said about God......
Helena ?

HELENA : Caesar......God has made flesh
part of his infinite and adorable redemption,
and when I say Caesar, it is all clear
because this is the very image of redemption.

CONSTANTIUS : Blessed one, what you say is as difficult
as to believe that your voice is able to exist
being so beautiful. But......are you a Christian ?
Do not say. I think that both Rome and I are come
into possession of a soul. Vision of glory,
I adore you, I love you ; my heart breaks with you.

HELENA : Caesar, most blessed and adorable Caesar !

(*THEIR HANDS TOUCH.*)

CONSTANTIUS : If there should be something that had my
power
and your spirit, he should alter the world. Rome
needed but such a redemption to be both
in earth and heaven ; it was heaven she lacked. O City,
O most adorable and most glorious City,
Rome in Love is something Rome has not known.
You are the mother of love.

(*HE KISSES HER.*)

HELENA : Love......love......O Caesar.

*(SHE FAINTS IN HIS ARMS. HE CATCHES HER.)*

CONSTANTIUS : Golden beatitude of beauty, a new City
    shall rise from you and me ; our two hearts
    making a future from this quality of greatness
    shall strew time with a fresh order of perfection,
    a holy wisdom, sprung from Colchester and Rome,
    redeemed flesh blazing with primordial glory—
    Love our first child, and our second child
    the tiaraed Augustus, woman and man in Victory.

*(HELENA RECOVERS HERSELF.)*

HELENA : Sweet my lord, let me go now.

CONSTANTIUS : Must you ? go then ; and if you are a Christian,
    which yet I must not know, but if you are,
    commend me to the God who made you lovely
    and set such lucid powers within your flesh
    as half would make me think he lived within you.
    Good-night, my Colchester.

HELENA :                Good-night, my Caesar.

    *(SHE WITHDRAWS.)*

CONSTANTIUS : Love is our first child ; if we have a second,
    I dedicate him to this hour. He shall
    draw a new doctrine into the heart of Rome,
    even if, to do so, he change the place of Rome.
    Gentlemen !

    *(THE KING, ETC., RETURN.)*

    Sir, we must alter our intention. Now—
    to-night—we must be gone. Command our horses.

    *(TO A SERVANT.)*

KING COLE : My lord—

CONSTANTIUS :         No evil : good, all good. Hark,
    I will say no more than—pardon and expect us.
    Sir, men take joy in men and women in women,
    friendship and delight of love, but this—a Christian ?

What do the Christians believe?—No, do not say.
It is not time yet; wait.  Good-night: our horses!

    *(THEY GO OUT.)*

THE ACCUSER: You do not, my lord Constantinople, smile
    to see the beginning of your greatness?  This man died
    at York: his son was Constantine, and a Christian—
    no-one knows why.

CONSTANTINOPLE:              Indeed no-one knows why.
    But in some exchange between the Omnipotence
    and man, in some such ravishing hour as this,
    when our incarnate and most courteous lord
    exhibits the actual unveiled beauty of flesh
    to eyes of love; making the love and the loving,
    the lover and the beloved, the beloved and the lover,
    into a glorious mystery of himself—
    might that not be an obscure reason in God?
    Brother, our lord is incarnate; you forget—
    and not a mirage in a desert of piety.
    The infidel has walled up Holy Wisdom,
    which this man's son first built, but a million lovers
    circulate Holy Wisdom through the world,
    to be spiritual sees of Christendom.  There is
    an apostolic tradition in the blood
    when the flood of the spirit takes it, as the water
    mingles with the precious and original blood.
    Speak, brothers.

CANTERBURY:           Man's room of earth and air
    is often gay through his gloom with miracles of sweet
                          play;
    he hears the birds or the poets, he sights
    the sea or architectural lines; he loves
    great designs; his rhythms turn holy rites:
    sense is one great defence against the Fall.

It has pleased God to throw a light thence
(as one of your poets said) on a world of greatness,
an invisible world, a world of absolute power.
For Eden wall is low and man's eyes look over
to see where the doves of Pentecost hover
through and about the giant tree of life,
rife with its twelve kinds of fruits ; Paradise
shoots rumours through his flesh and heavenly humours
through his soul.  Who witnesses thus ?

CHELMSFORD :                                    Brother and lord,
ask my fields and towns ; it is so still
as it was ere the first tribesmen found the ford
over Thames upwards.

CANTERBURY :                          Shrill is the call, shrill,
as then in the forests so now among the machines,
man hears in his working at a smile or a sunset or a
                                                    song.
Who hears sows ; where reaps he or where gleans ?

JERUSALEM : In me ; in the other gloom,
the long blank of the tomb that is no tomb
when all happiness parts from the broken hearts
when the insolent and inflamed horror sweeps
over man's Christendom of flesh, and leaps
teeth and claws on his heart ; the Lord Diocletian's
                                                    beasts
are but an image of this, when hell's persecution
rages everywhere and always through all peace—
pain along the nerves and along the lives
drives : everything is but a vision of pain :
who witnesses thus ?

CHELMSFORD :                              I again,
down through the docks of the fields and the docks of
                                                    the towns

till the heart rocks with the threat of the terror. Yet
I have set, holy ones, my will and my word beyond
all earthly words ; I bid my Christ to his bond.
Could he, if he wanted, rid himself of me for ever ?
Never ; it is mine to command and his to obey.
Pray, shall I ? this I say when I pray :
*Be quick, be quick ; it is I ; you love me ; come.*

THE ACCUSER : Ha, sweet, have I driven you to ground at
last ?

CHELMSFORD : Come, come ; lord and my love, come.

*(JERUSALEM COMES DOWN TO THE LOWER
STAGE. TWO SERAPHS CARRY IN FRONT
OF HIM A COVERED BURDEN.)*

### The Chorus.

Sing, my tongue, the glorious battle,
  Sing the ending of the fray ;
Now above the Cross, the trophy,
  Sound the loud triumphant lay :
Tell how Christ, the world's redeemer,
  As a victim won the day.

Faithful Cross, above all other
  One and only noble Tree !
None in foliage, none in blossom,
  None in fruit thy peer may be ;
Sweetest wood, and sweetest iron !
  Sweetest weight is hung on thee.

JERUSALEM : Christ our City, have pity on all barbarians,
  all tribal shriekings beyond the City,
  Docetists or Arians, denials of the Man or the God,
  the earth or the heaven, made one in one birth,
  one Passion, one Resurrection : make election,
  daughter.

CHELMSFORD :       I made it long since ; I will not leave
  anything out ; now I bring all to all.

JERUSALEM : Yet let some voice of yours speak while we show
  that the tale of the mystical legend may have its meaning,
  and Helena Empress be shown for all souls' queening.
  Shall it be Cedd ?

ST. CEDD : Not I ; choose rather
    some other worker who spread the news,
    one of your saints and children, a son
    of your district, your diocese—any ; name him.
CHELMSFORD : Light in the dim ways, flame in the heart's
                                   home,
    I call one who later was a bishop himself,
    but young gave tongue in me for a blessing,
    confessing in Little Easton the Christhood.
    Thomas Ken, come !.........and hear you him preach,
    as teaching his people on a May Day of festival.
          *(KEN ENTERS AND SPEAKS AS IF FROM*
          *HIS PULPIT TO HIS PARISHIONERS.)*
KEN : You are to consider, good people, that all the things
    that are said about our blessed Lord in Holy Scripture
    are said also about his way with the soul. For his work
    is threefold : what he did on earth, and what he does in
    the Church, and what he does in every soul which desires
    him to work upon it ; and these three manners of working
    agree in one. So that when we say that he is the Way,
    we mean it in these three kinds. And this I have very
    often expounded to you.

    But this is true too of those tales and legends which the
    Church recommends to her children, as is said concerning
    the Apocryphal Books in the articles of our own Church
    of England : 'and these the Church doth read for
    instruction of manners, though she doth not account
    them canonical.' Days of holy men are celebrated among
    us that we may remember them as examples to us.
    There are, besides these, certain days of observation—
    which are meant for our profit ; and this very Sunday
    on which we are met here is one of them. It is called in
    our Kalendar the Invention of the Cross, by which is
    meant the Discovery or Finding of that Cross on which

our holy Saviour died. We have been told that this very Cross, which was preserved by, as it were, miracle for many hundreds of years, was brought again to light by a pious woman, the Empress Helena, who was the mother of the first Christian Emperor Constantine. It was said once that she was an English woman and came from this very country of yours now called Essex, or the land of the East Saxons, but I think learned men say that this is not so and that she came first from certain parts beyond the Danube. But whatever this truth may be, still she was married to the Roman Caesar of Britain, and it is becoming, because of that old tale, and because of her place here, and because of her son who brought peace to the Church, and because of the grace that was shown her in the Discovery of the Holy Cross—it is proper, I say, good people of Essex, that you should consider what this Finding of the Cross means.

For first consider that she lived in great love and pleasantness with her husband the Caesar Constantius as long as God allowed them, and that after he died at York she did all that was in her power to guard and cherish and teach her son who was to be the great Emperor of all the world. But after this was done, and he gone to his own wars, she gave herself wholly up to God. And consider now with yourselves by how many pleasant-nesses God has shown his meaning to you also, and by how many proper strictnesses he has shown you that he will have you come to himself only. Consider this a little, I pray you.

> (*HE PAUSES. THE EMPRESS HELENA
> ENTERS, IN THE ROBES OF AN IMPERIAL
> WIDOW, ATTENDED BY SEVERAL WOMEN
> AND PRIESTS. SHE KNEELS IN PRAYER.*)

JERUSALEM : Helena.........Helena.

THE CHORUS : Helena !

(*SHE LISTENS, RISES, AND SEEMS TO SPEAK TO HER ATTENDANTS.*)

KEN : Now it was so that our good Lord, having determined to show grace to this holy matron, put it into her mind that she should make a journey through all the Empire of Rome until she came to Jerusalem ; which was very possible for her because she was a great lady, but is not at all so possible for you and me who are not the parents of Emperors. But are we not all called to take our journey to another Jerusalem, which is above ? and can we find any other way but by much care and spiritual travelling ? such as that holy lady had done in her heart before ever she began to understand the will of God towards her. And consider you now for a space the many toils and vexations that she endured on her journey, and we on ours, and the whole Church of God upon its own—of which we here in Essex are a small part.

(*HE PAUSES. HELENA, IN SOME STATE, BEGINS HER PASSAGE ROUND THE STAGE, MOVING ROUND WITH THE SUN, AND PASSING BY ROME AND CONSTANTINO-PLE.*)

ROME : Lady of old Rome, pass to old Jerusalem.

CONSTANTINOPLE : Mother of new Rome, pass to new Jerusalem.

(*SHE COMES NEAR JERUSALEM AND STANDS STILL.*)

KEN : But it is one thing to come where the Cross is and another thing to find the Cross. Trials and vexations are God's way of bringing us to God's holy place, that is to say, to the Jerusalem that is within our souls. But he brought Caiaphas to Jerusalem, and Pilate ; yes, they lived in it and were familiar with it. You may come to this Church where we are and know it, yes, kneel and stand up in it, and say thanks to God for it ; and all the while you shall be as far from that other Jerusalem as Judas was from Christ when he shouldered him in the crowd. That holy lady had found a Calvary in her heart before ever she came near it on earth. Consider therefore what speed you should be making now.

(*HE PAUSES. HELENA COMES UP TO JERUSALEM AND KNEELS. HE BLESSES HER. SHE STANDS UP, AND MOVES TOWARDS THE HIDDEN CROSS. A PACE OR TWO AWAY SHE STOPS. THE WHOLE TABLEAU IS RIGID.*)

KEN : But, O good people, how blessed are you if, having come to that Jerusalem, you do indeed find, by God's grace, the secret and hidden thing. For find you the Cross without you, as did that blessed lady, you shall find a precious, an inestimable treasure, the wood on which our Saviour rested without resting, the bloody, bloody wood he bedewed. But find you the Cross within you, as that blessed Empress also did, and you shall find Christ himself, Christ that is the Cross, and so holy, so sweet, so fresh and fragrant a Cross that you shall laugh to find how you have mistook him. For this Cross—but consider you this a little moment.

(*HELENA SIGNS. THE SERAPHS THROW BACK THE COVER. THE EMPRESS AND HER ATTENDANTS KNEEL.*)

KEN : This Cross is no longer an unwilling sacrifice, no, nor a difficult sacrifice ; it is not a slow duty, no, nor a quick duty ; nor anything at all but our most sweet and courteous Lord being to us a justification and a sanctification, and our very life itself ; and this is in all of you to be found as surely, O much more surely, than the Empress of Rome found the wood of the beams in Jerusalem. And it is this which saves, justifies, sanctifies the Church of God—all of you, and I, and that fortunate Helena, and her son, and her husband, and any and all men in all districts and dioceses; and the Church and all mankind has good cheer by this. And we in this land that was of the East Saxons and is now Essex, and belonged once to old Rome under Caesar and now to new Jerusalem in Christ; and especially you, my own people of Little Easton, rejoice we all to-day for the great and wonderful Invention of the Holy Cross, that Christ found for all us and we in him, and all souls that be by his most sweet manhood and foundation bound fast to him; and afterwards by his grace doubly born to him: and go we all forth thinking of this and praising him, without whom nothing had been at all for ever and ever. Amen.

*(HE GOES OUT, HELENA WITHDRAWING TO THE SIDE. THE SERAPHS SUPPORT THE CROSS.)*

THE WHOLE CHORUS :
> Bend thy boughs, O Tree of Glory !
> Thy relaxing sinews bend ;
> For awhile the ancient rigour
> That thy birth bestowed, suspend ;
> And the King of Heavenly Beauty
> On thy bosom gently tend !

JERUSALEM : Bend, Christian soul, the hard branches,
slowly loosen the rigid sinews ; flow
into the vital Christ-of-the-Cross. Where
have you been all this time but only here ?
this is at once indictment, judgement, and release,
when your Peace awakes through all moments at once.
This is that which is you.

CHELMSFORD :                    I know, as I knew
from Cedd's mouth first, and afterwards spoken
by others : I too have had children who said so
in emblems and images. Heavenly kinsmen, sound
some song of theirs, while I bound myself in his frame.
My Lord heard me call ; quickly he came.

ST. CEDD : Choose Francis Quarles, a chronologer of peace.

THE CHORUS :
> Ev'n like two little bank-dividing brooks,
> That wash the pebbles with their wanton
> > streams,
> And having rang'd and search'd a thousand
> > hooks,
> Meet both at length in silver-breasted Thames,
> Where in a greater current they conjoin :
> So I my best-beloved's am ; so he is mine.

Ev'n so we met and after long pursuit,
Ev'n so we join'd ; we both became entire ;
No need for either to renew a suit,
for I was flax and he was flames of fire :
Our firm-united souls did more than twine ;
So I my best-beloved's am ; so he is mine.

He is my Altar ; I, his Holy Place ;
I am his guest ; and he, my living food ;
I'm his by penitence ; he mine by grace ;
I'm his by purchase ; he is mine, by blood ;
He's my supporting elm ; and I his vine :
Thus I my best-beloved's am ; thus he is
                                    mine.

CHELMSFORD (leaning happily on the Cross) :
    O Grief, I take the Joy your grief brings ;
    Joy, what is Grief while that Joy lives ?
THE ACCUSER : Sweet lady, this is the answer to all.
JERUSALEM : Fair daughter, this is the truth of all.
CHELMSFORD : Blessed master, now I can love you right.

                  (*TO THE ACCUSER.*)

Blessed father, now I can see you right.

                  (*TO JERUSALEM.*)

Call them, all those that are I.
Call them, to be one pattern here with me.
THE CHORUS : Adeste, fideles, laetantes, triumphantes.

              (*ALL THE PERSONS ENTER.*)

CHELMSFORD (aspiring forward from the Cross) :
    Are you all here ?
ALL THE PERSONS : All ; all.
CHELMSFORD : Answer then, I for you and you for me—
    all you my past, all you my present, all

you invisible powers that shall be yet my future.
Say, shall I name the glory, in you and for you?

ALL : Lady, we name the glory, in you and for you.

CHELMSFORD : Say, shall I take the Cross, in you and for you

ALL : Lady, we take the Cross, in you and for you.

CHELMSFORD : Say, shall I melt to the Love, in you and for
you?

ALL : Lady, we melt to the Love, in you and for you.

JERUSALEM : Brother, finish your work.

(*HE RE-ASCENDS.*)

THE ACCUSER (laughing) : Do *I* shirk the Joy,
I who am God's true knowledge of all things made?
Come, beloved.

(*HE TAKES HER FROM THE CROSS.*)

CHELMSFORD : Dearest of all lovers!

(*THEY EMBRACE PASSIONATELY.*)

THE ACCUSER :                           Most sweet lady,
I have waited an hour, and yet an hour for this;
now I will lift you where we have willed : on,
on to the City, the Love between all lovers.

(*HE TAKES HER UP THE STEPS. AS SHE
COMES NEAR THE HEIGHT SHE PAUSES
AND LEANS OVER.*)

CHELMSFORD (calling to those below) :
Now, children of miracle, in you and for you!

ALL (including the heavenly persons and the Chorus) :
Now, lady of miracle, in you and for you!

(*SHE REACHES THE HEIGHT. THE WHOLE
COMPANY BEGIN THE TE DEUM. DURING
THE FIRST FIVE VERSES, CHELMSFORD
MEETS AND EMBRACES THE SEES.*)

HE WHOLE COMPANY : We praise thee, O God : we acknowledge thee to be the Lord.

All the earth doth worship thee : the Father everlasting.

To thee all Angels cry aloud : the Heavens, and all the Powers therein.

To thee Cherubin, and Seraphin : continually do cry,

Holy, Holy, Holy : Lord God of Sabaoth ;

> (*SHE TURNS BACK TO THE ACCUSER AND GIVES HIM HER HAND.*)

Heaven and earth are full of the Majesty : of thy Glory.

> (*THE ACCUSER TAKES HER TO THE CENTRE ; THE SEES GROUP ROUND THE TWO OF THEM.*)

The glorious company of the Apostles : praise thee.

The goodly fellowship of the Prophets : praise thee.

The noble army of Martyrs : praise thee.

The holy Church throughout all the world : doth acknowledge thee ;

The Father : of an infinite Majesty ;

Thine honourable, true ; and only Son ;

Also the Holy Ghost : the Comforter.

> (*CHELMSFORD TAKES A STEP FORWARD, THE ACCUSER CLOSE BEHIND HER, ON HER RIGHT.*)

Thou art the King of Glory : O Christ.